THE
BUSINESS OF
ASSERTIVENESS

THE BUSINESS OF ASSERTIVENESS

Rennie Fritchie and Maggie Melling

BBC BOOKS

Published by BBC Books,
a division of BBC Enterprises Limited,
Woodlands, 80 Wood Lane, London W12 0TT

First published 1991

Text © 1991 by Development Associates Group Limited
Kenneth Pollard House
5–19 Cowbridge Road East
Cardiff CF1 9AB

Cartoons by Martin Brown

© 1991 by BBC Enterprises Ltd

ISBN 0 563 36196 4

Set in 10/12 pt Times Roman by Ace Filmsetting Ltd, Frome, Somerset
Printed and bound in Great Britain by Clays Ltd, St Ives Plc
Cover printed by Clays Ltd, St Ives Plc

Contents

The Authors

RENNIE FRITCHIE is a consultant in organisation development, management development and personal development. Her work in this field covers all sectors – public, private, voluntary, trade unions and education. She works internationally in Europe and the USA and has a special working relationship with Tall Poppies, a New Zealand consultancy. Since 1988 she has additionally held the post of Chair of Gloucester Health Authority which is a part of the National Health Service.

MAGGIE MELLING is a consultant with a personnel background, she has a wide experience of training and development in a broad range of organisations. Originally from Yorkshire, Maggie lives in the Cotswolds combining family and work responsibilities in as balanced a way as she can.

Acknowledgements

In writing this book we have had help and support from a number of sources and so we would like to recognise that and to say thank you to:

- **Pam Blanchett** for typing, co-ordinating and managing a smooth process.
- **Suzanne Webber and Deborah Taylor** of BBC Books for clear objectives, helpful guidelines and flexible deadlines.
- **The Fritchie Family** Andrew, Eric and Fiona
- **The Melling Family** Tim, Rebecca and Paul for their support, encouragement and constructive criticism.
- **Friends and colleagues** for their contributions and understanding.
- **Martin Brown** for his excellent cartoons and for his friendly help.

We have written this book to meet a real need and we hope that it will be used in an active and interactive way.

We have shared our thoughts, theories and experiences and we would be delighted to hear from you, following this interactive process and practising what we preach.

We wish you every success with this business of assertiveness.

Rennie Fritchie and Maggie Melling

Introduction

The constantly changing world of work requires organisations to be leaner, fitter and more demanding of their management than ever before – and only those managers who respond to the challenge will be successful. Every manager and member of staff is facing a new list of 'must do and be' to accomplish, it often looks a lot like this:

They must be able to:

- handle conflict creatively
- cope with stress
- work across boundaries
- prevent problems rather than solve them
- give and receive feedback positively
- ask intelligent questions

They must be:

- a self-starter
- a self-motivator
- a visionary
- a creative thinker
- an effective decision maker
- an integrated team member

They must also know how to be customer aware and quality conscious. All this with less time and far fewer resources.

This strikes us as a modern list of 'six impossible tasks to accomplish before breakfast'! Highly desirable but very often little or no help is given as to *how* this can all be accomplished.

This book is a *How-to* book with many ideas, examples and suggestions. Most of all it is a practical guide in how to:

- tackle difficult situations

- handle and avoid conflict

- say *what* you want, in the *way* that you want at the *time* that you want. (So many of our best replies come two hours late and from someone else!)

This book is called *The Business of Assertiveness* because the main focus is on how to be more effective in the work place. However, as we rarely behave in one way at work and another at home, it has a wider understanding and application.

We do not guarantee that this book will change your life – only *you* can do that. However, it will give you a range of choices instead of leaving you feeling stuck, put down, or overwhelmingly angry, and it will give you the opportunity to practise the techniques to be able to make your choices.

1 The Business of Assertiveness

We are all very different as human beings; each one of us is an original! Given this, it would not be appropriate to have one stock answer or approach for all people in all situations. It is important to understand what makes us angry or passive and to have a number of choices about how to handle difficult situations effectively. A number of responses may be right for us, taking account of our age, gender, temperament and current situation.

What is Assertiveness?

Assertiveness has become a familiar word today. It is used to convey meaning to a body of knowledge and techniques in much the same way as negotiation, leadership and decision-making are used in the world of training.

The recent growth in the development of assertiveness has its origins in the United States of America during the 1960s and 1970s. During this time, tremendous changes were taking place in society. In particular, the new climate of freedom and equality meant that it was now possible for people who had previously had only limited opportunities to now have access to a very different way of life. In many areas of society, people were being encouraged to strive for a better way of life and for more independence. It quickly became clear, however, that there was quite a difference between having *access* to the opportunity and being able to use it by having the *ability* to speak up and be taken seriously, and to do it without damaging the rights of others.

Within organisations people who had responsibility for the development and training of personnel were faced with very different behaviours, ranging from aggressive to passive and including a whole range of attitudes. In order to help people to work effectively together, these developers began to explore new ways of helping people to become more competent, self-confident and assertive.

■ *Who is assertiveness for?*

Assertiveness is for everyone. It is *not* merely remedial training for disadvantaged groups or individuals. It is developmental training which enables people of all ages and at all career stages to be more confident and able to say the right thing, at the right time and in the right way with a much higher possibility of achieving the right outcome. Many organisations now integrate working with assertiveness into their mainstream management development programmes along with problem-solving and staff supervision.

All too often technical training is given priority over personal effectiveness. This can result in people having technical expertise but no real ability to deal with people in a clear and fair way. By balancing technical training with assertiveness training it is possible to develop people who not only know *what* to do but also *how* to do it by working *with* people.

Assertiveness is for:

- men and women
- all ethnic groups
- all kinds of organisations – high tech and low tech
- public sector
- industry
- commerce
- voluntary sector
- finance
- education sector

And moreover, it is for *you* too!

■ *Why is assertiveness important?*

There are two major reasons why it is important for people to learn how to be assertive and therefore how to say what they really think, want or feel without denying the thoughts, needs or feelings of others.

The first and most obvious reason is that with the ability to be assertive people are much more likely to get more of what they want. Very often it is this reason which leads people to the subject of assertiveness in the first place and is in itself a worthwhile goal. However, even with the ability to be assertive, people will not always be one hundred per cent successful in getting absolutely everything that they want.

The second major reason for people learning to be assertive is quite simply this: to feel good about themselves and their behaviour. This is just as important as achieving successful outcomes from difficult situations, although initially it may be less obvious. Some problem situations can be anticipated and planned for, however, many difficult situations occur quite unexpectedly. Either way, there are usually two different questions we ask ourselves. The first is – What actually happened? The second is – How did I handle it?

Around about the time of the event it is what actually happened that often remains uppermost in our minds, but, what we tend to remember later is not the event itself, but how we handled it.

In difficult situations, people often react by being aggressive, saying too much too loudly and often overreacting and then regretting it later. Alternatively, they become passive, silent, holding back, saying and doing nothing and afterwards thinking 'what should I have done?' or 'what could I have said?' and feeling bad about themselves and unhappy with their performance. In both circumstances, these inadequate handlings of the situation usually reinforce a person's poor view of themselves and leads to a lack of self-respect. Take a common example of someone jumping the queue and stealing 'your' car parking space. Aggressive people can shout, swear, be sarcastic and use meaningful gestures, but they will not change the parking situation and the anger will still be with them hours later.

Passive people are likely to sit quietly, feel angry and fume inwardly, thinking of all the things they would like to do but doing none of them and feeling angry with themselves for failing to act. Again, this inward anger and self disappointment is still there hours later. In both cases, if this is their usual way of dealing with problem issues, it will just be adding to their already formed inadequate image of themselves – 'yet again I blew up' or 'yet again I did nothing'. By being assertive in this situation it is possible for them to change both the outcome and feel good about the way they handled the situation. One assertive response would be to speak to the queue jumper as follows:

> '*I know that it is hard to park here and it may be that you did not see the line of cars waiting for a space, however, I was at the front of the line and feel upset at losing this place. I have come to ask you to move to the end of the queue.*'

You may get an angry reply (aggressive) or be ignored (passive), or you may get an apology and your car parking space. It has been known! What you will definitely get is a strong feeling of self-respect for having tackled it in a straightforward way, and even if you do not get your parking space, at least it won't spoil the rest of your day!

So it is important to be assertive not only to get more of what you want but also to feel better about yourself and your behaviour.

Why assertiveness is not easy

In both philosophy and action, assertiveness is simple. But being simple does not, unfortunately, make it easy to put into practice. If we had all learned how to be assertive as young children it might be both simple and easy to be assertive as adults. The reality for most of us is that our development has been affected by both CULTURE and GENDER which result in our taking particular actions and learning particular types of behaviour. Men are often encouraged to be more aggressive and women to be conciliatory and to keep everyone happy – except, often, themselves. This starts early in life when boys are told to 'hit someone back if they hit you' whereas girls may be encouraged to 'go and make friends' after a row.

This difference in gender behaviour starts at birth and continues through life. It can be obvious, like the difference in toys which are manufactured and marketed for boys and girls or less obvious, like the tasks young people are given in the home, different expectations at school, job segregation in the world of paid employment and many other aspects in society at large. The message imparted to girls and boys, women and men are still fairly clear today – men are encouraged to:

- be tough
- be strong
- be in the lead
- be in control
- not back down
- give as good as you get
- show no weakness
- win if you can, never mind the cost

This is a tall order and leaves little room for subtlety, sensitivity or reaching joint agreement and it can cause stress and strain.

Women are still encouraged to:

- be gentle
- follow
- be compassionate
- put others before themselves
- share
- not to argue
- not to get angry

This makes it difficult for women to speak up or ask for things, especially for herself, or to be direct and handle conflicts. All this, of course, can also cause stress and strain.

Certainly, not all men are aggressive and not all women are passive; society, however, often expects and rewards these kinds of behaviours from women and men.

Culture, too, has a part in preventing assertiveness from being easy. In some countries bartering, even arguing, is a way of life. In others like Britain, queueing up and waiting patiently for your turn is the order of the day. It is important to understand these cultural expectations and demands, and to recognise the limitations they place on people.

We all have a range of feelings and behaviours, yet we often have our own individual style which is picked up by other people and interpreted. Have a look at the chart on page 20 which describes three common approaches. In the chart we look at passive, aggressive and assertive positions from four points of view:

- our view of ourselves
- other people's view of us
- our feelings
- our actions

See if there is one way which describes your approach more accurately than another. Check with a friend to see if their assessment tallies with your own!

How can you benefit from becoming more assertive?

- You will manage your time and stress levels more effectively by setting realistic limits.

- You can influence others by stating your preferences and opinions clearly and in an appropriate, easily-heard way.

- You will learn more quickly what others think or would prefer (by active listening, clarifying, checking out and reflecting back).

- You will deal with problems more easily (by being clear about the key issues and priorities before focusing on the solutions).

	PASSIVE	AGGRESSIVE	ASSERTIVE
Self view	I am a quiet person with very little to contribute.	I am a tough person who should be listened to. I always know best.	I am an individual whose views and thoughts can make a contribution.
Other's views	This is an unconfident and unsure person, always happy to sit back and let others take the lead. They are content to go, or be put, last.	This is an over-confident person who will bully others to get their own way believing they have more 'rights' than them. They must always come first.	This is a confident person who regularly demonstrates a balancing of their own needs and wants of others.
Feelings	I regularly feel shy, frustrated, depressed, questioning, stressed, tired, stuck, hopeless, lost and inadequate, helpless, out of place, unhappy, downtrodden and **guilty.**	I regularly feel angry, irritated, hot and bothered, furious, blocked, unappreciated, out of control, watchful, attacked.	I regularly feel assured, competent, confident, happy, able to deal well with conflict.
Actions	I say no when I want to say *yes.* I can't say *no* when I'm being taken advantage of, I dither in decision-making. I will avoid conflict at all costs.	I enjoy a good fight, I like to win at everything. I rarely consult, believing actions are more important than words. I believe that people enjoy being told what to do.	I recognise my own rights to be: listened to, consulted, involved in decision-making. I believe I am responsible for upholding those rights, and I believe that the same rights are due equally to others.

- As you become more honest and direct, you will emerge as the unique individual you are. This will help other people to be honest and direct too.

- You will feel more confident and in charge of your life as you consider your needs and make choices that work for you and others.

■ *Benefits for your company*

- Assertive individuals working in teams will be more effective, both in achieving their aims and working well together.

- The organisation will be an enjoyable place to work and therefore recruitment of highly skilled workers will be easier.

- More innovation as employers feel their contributions are welcomed.

- Staff retention will be higher.

- Senior Managers will receive specific direct feedback linked to suggested actions from their junior colleagues.

- Once it is recognised that people do make mistakes (and are responsible for sorting them) less energy is used up on cover ups and pretence.

How assertive are you?

In theory, all organisations will be effective and smooth running if:

- there are good clear objectives
- efficient planned systems
- adequate resources

In practice, even with the very best objectives, systems and resources, all is not plain sailing.

It is worth looking at meetings, appraisals and ways of dealing with people to see the kind of behaviour that causes frustration, misunderstanding and which can lead to long term problems.

Meetings

In the meetings you attend how many of the people present do the following:

- listen silently and don't ask questions when what is being said is unclear?
- only listen to the first part of what is being said and then cut in with their opinion?
- wait for others to make their points for them?
- begin to state their case and if there isn't instant approval, change direction entirely or drift to an end?
- when the meeting has lost its way, allow it to drift on in a mixture of directions without being able to get it back on track or end it?
- let one or two people 'take over' the meeting and manipulate the outcome?

Appraisals

Appraising is part of everyday work life and a formal appraisal is a good opportunity for good communication and clear understanding about job performance and future development needs. However, all too often the following occurs: The people being appraised:

- take defensive stances and justify and rationalise past events.
- attack their appraiser for being unfair.
- get unpleasant surprises because the appraiser has been avoiding giving direct feedback all year.
- feel the whole thing is cosmetic because real issues are never addressed.

How often do the people who are doing the appraising:

- use the interview as an opportunity to criticise without giving any positive feedback?
- hint indirectly at events or interpretations of behaviour without being specific?

- criticise the person in blanket terms and never their behaviour, e.g. 'You're a bad manager' or 'You're a poor communicator'?
- become angry with the appraisee and stop listening?
- allow the interview to drift to an end without any clear understanding or agreement about new objectives and without the criteria to judge whether the new objectives have been met?

■ *Dealing with people*

The culture of an organisation can often be interpreted in the way people deal with each other – both dealing with visitors or customers and internally in the way staff treat each other.

How many of the following occur in relation to the groups in your organisation?

Visitors and customers

- There are no clear signs for visitors to find their way.
- The reception area is hidden away with off-putting barriers e.g. closed doors, sliding glass windows always shut.
- There is an excluding atmosphere inside the reception area, staff talk and smile with one another and ignore outsiders.
- Visitors are left waiting for long periods with no information about what is happening.

Staff

- Groups of people whisper in the corridors.
- Cliques are formed at coffee times and lunch times and there is very little mixing between departments.
- People regularly say one thing to your face and another behind your back.
- There is a great deal of 'scapegoating' going on with blame being attributed in an unhelpful way.

- There are regular 'rows' between individuals or departments with 'sides' being taken throughout the organisation.

- Many people say they are one person at work and a very different one at home, they feel they have to pretend, protect and role-play to be accepted.

All these behaviours are time wasting, counter-productive and expensive. The cost can be financial to the organisation and personal to individuals.

It is not easy for one person to change the whole organisation, however, a good first step is to rate your own assertive behaviour and then actively work on being more assertive.

Try filling in the following questionnaire as a first check on your own assertiveness. Very few of us will score as highly as we would like to. Initially, however, it is important to be honest and fair in your assessment of yourself so that you can get a clear idea of your areas for improvement.

Questionnaire: How assertive are you?

Answer the following 20 questions, putting a tick in the box which most accurately describes you.

	Often	*Sometimes*	*Rarely*	*Never*
1 In a difficult meeting, with tempers running high, I am able to speak up with confidence.				√
2 If I am unsure of something I can easily ask for help.		√		
3 If someone is being unfair and aggressive I can handle the situation confidently.			√	
4 When someone is being sarcastic at my expense or at the expense of others, I can speak up without getting angry.			√	

	Often	Sometimes	Rarely	Never
5 If I am being put down or patronised I can raise the issue directly without being aggressive.			✓	
6 If I believe I am being taken for granted, I am able to draw attention to it without sulking or getting upset.				✓
7 If someone asks my permission to do something I would prefer them not to e.g. smoke, I can say no without feeling guilty.			✓	
8 If I am asked my opinion about something I feel quite comfortable to give it even if I think my opinion will not be a popular one.			✓	
9 I can deal easily and effectively with senior people.				✓
10 When given faulty or substandard goods in a shop or restaurant I can state my case well without attacking the other person.				✓
11 When an important opportunity is in the offing I can speak up on my own behalf.				✓
12 When I can see things going wrong I can draw attention to it early without waiting until it is a potential disaster.			✓	

	Often	Sometimes	Rarely	Never
13 When I have bad news to give I can do it calmly and without excessive worry.				√
14 If I want something I can ask for it in a direct, straightforward way.		√		
15 When someone isn't listening to what I'm saying, I can get my point across without getting strident or feeling sorry for myself.			√	
16 When someone misunderstands me, I can point it out without feeling guilty or making the other person look small.			√	
17 When I disagree with the majority views I can state my case without apologising or getting high-handed.				√
18 I take deserved criticism well.		√		
19 I give compliments without being embarrassed or sounding like empty flattery.			√	
20 When I get angry, I can express my point of view without becoming judgemental or feeling I've let myself down.			√	

How to score

Give yourself:

5 points for *often*
2 points for *sometimes*
1 point for *rarely*
0 points for *never*

75–100 – You are confident and assertive in your approach to situations.

50–75 – Although you can be assertive you would benefit further from working with assertiveness.

25–50 – You are unable to be consistent in your assertive behaviour.

 0–25 – You need to do some considerable work to develop assertive behaviour.

2 The imposter syndrome

Sometimes it is hard to be assertive because it is hard to be sure who we really are and what we really want to be. Many people feel inadequate at work. Even if others have a high opinion of you your own opinion may not match up. As a result you can begin to feel like a fake. This can lead to the Imposter Syndrome.

The Imposter Syndrome can be found to some degree in all organisations. When it is rife it becomes dangerous, not only for the individuals but also for the organisation as a whole.

We see it as a natural phenomenon which most of us experience when we are in new, unfamiliar situations and where there are very real expectations of us, for example, when you first take up a new job. You've won, beat the competition and you now have the job, the title, the salary, the car, the office with *double* pedestal desk, two and a half windows, carpet, secretary, expense account and car parking space! What you *don't* have is the certainty that you *are* the best person for the job! All around you people assume you know about things you've never heard of, they think that you:

- understand deeply the few things you have dimly grasped;
- have the *answers* to questions which you are still struggling to define;
- are somehow a living embodiment of your new title;
- are up to date with all the privileged information;
- know all about the company, its culture and the job history.

All the while, you are waiting to be found out for the Imposter you are; for someone to tap you on the shoulder and expose your inadequacies, shortcomings and weaknesses to the public at large. It is the 'if I'm doing so well, how come I feel such a failure?' experience. When this happens in a new job or situation, we have a choice; we can either put energy and effort into finding out what we need to know, understand and be able to do in order to be as good as people already think we are. Or we can skim the surface with buzz words and network our contacts in order to continue to look good and evade discovery. To get away with it! It is this second strategy which in the long term has such disastrous results for people and their organisations. This leads to pretence and blustering, stress and bravado. A well packaged individual who will pass in the short term and who may even get promoted on the strength of it but who erodes from within and eventually crumbles. Picture the people-strength of an organisation if enough Imposters rise to the top: quality will not be sustainable under any kind of pressure, crises will never be resolved, decisions not made and the whole fabric of the organisation eventually becomes thin and undernourished.

Identifying an imposter

Imposters are very hard to spot from above. After all, they are experts in creating a good impression and giving the answers that senior people want to hear rather than the facts that seniors need to know. They are also good at taking the credit for the work of colleagues and subordinates. Staff who work *for* an imposter are usually the first to spot them. They experience the lack of direction or severe gaps of knowledge and understanding. It is always different to live with someone and experience them in the round than to witness a short sustainable performance.

The next group to spot the chronic imposter is their colleagues or peers. They can tell the difference between a sporadic contributor and a lightweight, and those whose contribution is of true value. So those in charge are usually the last to know! You can see it would be hard to spot expert camouflage. It is also sometimes hard to spot a chronic imposter if you have tendencies in that direction yourself. You don't have enough depth to do the diagnosis and you have a lot invested in the *status quo*, as the discovery of one imposter might lead to another!

Some organisations have whole stratas of imposters. At the top or middle management level, or in individual specialist departments, who can blind everyone with their own brand of science. Imposters are rarely common at supervisory or junior management level – they would not survive, it is as they rise up the levels of the organisation that they begin to thrive!

Coping with imposters

If it is bad for an organisation to suffer from this syndrome, it is not much fun for the individuals either. The sheer strain of maintaining an exterior, warding off close encounters to avoid discovery and seeking every opportunity to shine, produces extreme stress on top of an already low self-esteem. Remember, the biggest bullies are often the biggest cowards. It is important to have the ability to:

- ask for information and for help in interpretation;
- make mistakes and learn from them (one senior company director always asks this question when recruiting senior staff: 'What is the biggest mistake you have made at work, how did it come about and what did you learn from it?').

If someone at senior level can think of no mistakes, then the inference taken is either they have made them and prefer to hide and forget them, so they have been wasted mistakes or they have genuinely never made a mistake, and so would be very unpredictable in the face of crisis or disaster – not a tested asset to the team.

So you can see the Imposter Syndrome has no benefits and very real consequences for both individuals and organisations. We believe the best way to avoid the Imposter Syndrome is to have the ability to be assertive so that even in new or difficult situations there is a real and positive alternative to faking it.

Arthur Jones, ex big-game hunter and rattlesnake collector, founder of Nautilus Sports Industries, says:

'Success comes from good judgement
Good judgement comes from experience
Experience comes from bad judgements!'

3 Masquerade

The Imposter Syndrome is bad enough in itself but we complicate life even further by adapting a range of different roles and wearing the matching mask in order to get by and be acceptable.

This lack of reality makes assertive behaviour very difficult. As assertiveness must come out of us, our personality and character, and not be reduced to trite phrases and false acting.

Almost as soon as we are born we start taking up a role and playing a part because somewhere in our lives there is someone who lets us know what they want from us and who they want us to be. Some of these masks we pick up for a while and then put down, others stay with us all our lives. Here are just some of the many masks which people can wear:

■ *Hapless, Helpless Harry/Helen*

These people behave like ineffectual victims who can't seem ever to do anything for themselves. They are endlessly accident prone and because they are so good at looking pathetic they usually get the help they think they need. The benefit of this mask is that they rarely disappoint anyone except themselves as so little is expected of them.

The drawback is that there is very little, if any, respect from other people and a whole series of rescuers are required in order to manage day-to-day living.

■ Bombastic, Bullying Brenda/Bruce

This is a colourful vivid mask in primary colours, usually worn when people want to get their own way and don't mind letting everyone else know about it. It is often used against smaller people in order to make someone feel big. Their motto is 'When unsure of your ground, go right ahead and bully!' The benefit of this mask is that it can be a quick way of getting your own way.

The drawback is that it is not usually successful in the longer term, and these people have few genuine friends.

■ Always Agreeable Annie/Alan

This mask is a good way of avoiding conflict. Smiling and saying 'yes' to everything and everyone can keep the working climate pleasant. The benefit of this mask is that people tend to like you and are glad, initially, to have you around.

The drawback is that you can quickly become exploited and are often dismissed as a lightweight who has nothing of substance to contribute. Others also feel guilty about their exploiting of you and so in the longer term begin to avoid you.

■ Rescuer Roger/Rita

This mask is one which, on the face of it, seems to be of real benefit to others. This person is always there to pick up the pieces, look after others and save the day. They tend to be constantly involved in the lives of others going from one crisis situation to another. Disasters draw them like magnets! The benefit is they are never short of friends – hapless, helpless Harrys and Helens positively seek them out. The drawback is that they are so involved in everyone else's lives they have little time for a life of their own. In a work environment it can have a dual effect. They can make mountains out of molehills and so divert positive energy into perpetuating negative situations. In addition, they can fall victim themselves when their own work or career takes a permanent back seat in favour of everyone else's needs.

■ Expert Edna/Ernie

This mask is the 'I know it all, been there, done it, let me tell you all about it,' mask. It is very irritating for colleagues. They are the best 'self-listeners' we know. Whatever the conversation they can turn it round in an instant to themselves and launch straight into expert advice. There are few benefits to this mask, it may initially gain attention but it soon wears off.

The drawbacks to this mask are numerous. People switch off around you and don't listen to the important contributions which you do make.

■ Jokey Jack/Janice

The comic's mask is a good way to deflect attention from the important or the serious. A smile and a witty comment can keep you in the driving seat and can focus attention on trivia making someone else the butt of your jokes. This is a good way to hide true feelings and to disguise a thoughtful mind. The benefits are that you remain the centre of attention and your vulnerability can remain a secret.

The drawbacks are that you remain 'light' entertainment and never have the opportunity to grow and develop – it's hard to keep a fixed smile in place.

These are just some of the masks which we wear. If we are to be ourselves and not Imposters and Masqueraders, it is important to learn to work with assertiveness.

PART TWO

1 Transactional Analysis

We have defined assertiveness as saying 'the right thing at the right time, in the right way, to the right person'. It all sounds simple when we think about it as a concept, or when we use it to help other people to solve their problems. The big test, however, is whether we can look at our own concerns, difficulties, and awkward situations with people, as a part of our working and personal lives and then use assertiveness to start leading more effective and more rewarding lives because of our approach. Although this book will give much practical emphasis on learning how to work with assertiveness, it is helpful to spend some time thinking about your own life so far.

- How you have developed your current approach.
- The specific situations and people that you find most difficult.
- The patterns of behaviour in yourself you most want to change or develop.

Ask yourself these questions:

1 Do I ever think that I am communicating in one way and later learn that others see me in a completely different way?
2 Do I ever ask a question at a meeting and then feel about two years old?
3 Do I ever tell someone off and then feel like kicking myself for it later?

4 Do I ever use the same technique to get what I want from my boss that I used as a child with my parents?
5 Do I often find myself being defensive about my ideas or points of view?
6 Do I feel that I have to take care of too many people who should be taking care of themselves?
7 Do I see myself as calm, cool and collected most of my working day?
8 Do I suddenly have a bright idea that seems to solve a problem?

Everyone has experienced some of these feelings or situations at some time or other. An important concept linked with effective, assertive behaviour is the analysis of transactions between people, that is, the different ways that people communicate with each other. Dr Eric Berne developed Transacational Analysis, or TA as it is usually known, to help people understand and improve their communication with others. In this book we will only use a small part of his theory in order to give some insight into communication behaviour. According to TA we can observe quite different and distinct types of behaviour which seem to come from different sources within ourselves. These three 'ego states' are called:

- PARENT

- ADULT

- CHILD

We are all a mixture of the different 'ego states'. Different situations may trigger a particular response out of one main state. By recognising these behaviours in ourselves, we can:

- start to understand why we get the reactions we do from other people, and

- start to change any behaviour that is damaging or ineffective.

Parent

Our Parent behaviour comes from what we observed as children in our parents and in other figures of authority. It is the concept that parents are:

- powerful
- responsible
- in charge
- always right
- not subject to the same rules as children
- not having to justify or to explain
- not necessarily even having to be fair

In our outward behaviour the Parent state is divided into two parts: CRITICAL PARENT and NURTURING PARENT.

Critical Parent

Critical Parent behaviour can be seen in transactions between people when one or both of them are laying down the law, or lecturing, or hiding behind regulations, or refusing to negotiate or compromise, for example:

1 'When I *tell you* I want something done, I mean *I want* it done now.'
2 'You *should* be coming up with solutions not problems.'
3 'Going for that promotion is a joke, you've got no chance.'
4 'You *ought* to have achieved a higher standard of presentation skills than this, you've let yourself and me down badly.'

Words like *ought, should, must* are real indicators of Critical Parent behaviour.

Nurturing Parent

Nurturing Parent behaviour, the other facet of the Parent state, is the caring, concerned behaviour where a person gives encouragement and support, shows warmth and affection, is sometimes over nurturing and therefore eventually becomes overwhelming.

For example:

1 'You were wonderful, I thought you did that really well, I was so pleased for you. I'm you're biggest fan.'
2 'If you are really worried about the meeting I'll go for you.'
3 'I think this promotion is a little early in your career and it might prove to be too much for you, much better to be patient and wait for something a little less demanding.'

Adult

Adult behaviour is the reasonable, calm, thoughtful behaviour that comes from an ability to think clearly through difficult issues to an effective workable solution. Adult behaviour means negotiating, not bullying, reaching a good solution, not caving in or steamrolling others, self-evaluating, responding reasonably and not reacting unreasonably. It also involves the ability to recognise and channel feelings by not allowing them to explode as well as recognising that the needs, feelings and positions of both yourself and others are of equal importance. Adult behaviour is assertive behaviour. For example:

1 'I can see that this promotion is important to you. I think it would be useful to match the job needs with your experience and quality and then make a final decision about your application.'
2 'I know that the time pressures on this order are very important and that we must meet your deadlines. I also want to maintain our high standards of innovative design and quality and I'd like to agree a schedule which will balance our requirements well.'

Child

The Child behaviour is divided into two main areas: Free Child and Adapted Child.

Free Child

Free Child behaviour is unbound by any limits or protocol, it is a straight, uncomplicated, uninhibited response which is often loud, energetic and exuberant. It is about doing what we feel like doing without any real thought beyond the immediate action. It can be fun, but it can also be thoughtless. Those of us with a strong free child are also often superb lateral thinkers. An energetic free child response would be, for example: 'I've got a really brilliant idea, it would totally transform the service we can give to our customers and it's so simple, all we need to do is . . .' etc.

Little Professor

Little Professor is part of Free Child; it is the creative, intuitive and curious element in our personality and behaviour. It is different from Adult behaviour in that it can operate without reasoning and often relies on intuition and even wild imagination in coming to decisions.

■ *Adapted Child*

Your Adapted Child developed when you learned to change or adapt your feelings or behaviour in response to the world around you. We start off as 'free' in our approach to life. With all the Critical and Nurturing Parent behaviour around us however, we soon adapt this natural way of being in order to accommodate the behaviour of others. It's through such adaptations that we become socialised, to share, to take turns, to be friendly. We must learn these skills to get along socially, saying 'please', and 'thank you' and 'I'm sorry', but the Adapted Child behaviour can be the most troublesome part of our personality. It is the constrained, learned behaviour that results from feelings of frustration, lack of control and inadequacy. It is behaviour which has been adapted in response to Critical Parent behaviour by, for example, complying reluctantly, by sulking or by avoiding a situation.

In Adapted Child behaviour people may try to please everyone or to turn their backs on people with problems, or to put off work until a deadline passes. The Adapted Child part of us is the part that feels less powerful than others resulting in our being:

- frightened before speaking in front of a group
- depressed when someone criticises our work
- hurt or angry when things don't go our way at a meeting
- anxious when important deadlines confront us.

'I was stunned when they moved me after I've been in the department only six months, and I was doing so well, it's not fair. I have to move, I have no choice, but if they think I'm going to give my all in this department, they've had it, I'm strictly a nine-to-five person from now on.'

With a little practice and a basic understanding of the Parent, Adult, Child outlined above, it isn't too difficult to start using TA to understand your own responses to other people, both at work and in your personal life. Once you begin to identify your own ego strengths it's easy to recognise the Parent, Adult, Child state of others. The following table may help you to begin this process.

	Controlling Parent	Nurturing Parent	Adult	Natural Child	Adapted Child
Words	Bad, should, ought, don't, must	Good, nice, well done, there, there, there	How? Why? Who? Yes, No	Fun, want, mine	Can't, won't wish, please, thank you
Gestures and postures	Pointing finger, pounding table, shaking head	Open arms, head and shoulder patting	Straight posture, level eye-contact	Energetic, loose-limbed, casual	Slumped, dejected, nail-biting, eyelash-fluttering
Tone of voice	Sneering, condescending	Loving, encouraging, concerned	Calm, clear, even, confident	Loud, free, easy, open	Whining, sulky, defiant, aggressive
Facial expression	Scowling, hostile, disapproving, frowning	Smiling	Thoughtful, alert	Joyful, twinkling	Fearful, pouting, wide-eyed, innocent

Once you can recognise the ego state, it is possible to develop the ability to switch states in order to move from being a caring Parent to an analytical Adult to a fun-loving Child without too much difficulty. Some of us find this easier than others. Often people do have favourite ego states and tend to stick with those, for example:

- some people are always criticising others or helping others – the constant parent

- some people continue to analyse and prefer facts to feelings – the constant adult

- some people operate with strong feeling all the time consumed with anger, aggression, guilt or anxiety – the constant child.

If you rigidly respond from only one ego state, however, it can cause serious problems – both for you and for those people who you interact with. Flexibility is the key to effectiveness; if one approach isn't working, try another. Be aware that if you approach someone in a Critical Parent mode, the most likely response will be Adapted Child, and the other way round. In business, the most appropriate response is usually as Adult, although, of course, there will be occasions when you will choose an alternative ego state in order to be effective.

2 Analyse your Power

An effective way of understanding your relationships and 'transactions' in work and in your personal life is to create a profile of them in diagram form – this process is called power-netting – it is a visual analysis of the who, what and why of the way you operate with the people around you.

Creating a work power-net is worthwhile for a number of reasons:

- Getting things done effectively and efficiently will contribute to good career progress within your organisation.

- Organisations have cultures – preferred ways of doing things, ways of treating people, valued ideas and philosophies, acceptable ways of thinking. If you want to make sure that the culture reflects *your* values and interests, it is important to gain, and effectively use, organisational power.

There are different ways in which people in organisations are powerful, and therefore, the ability to influence the direction and progress (or otherwise) of the organisation and individuals within it. Most people have some power in one form or another – organisational power-politics is seldom a one-way system. It can be useful to think of power as 'power in-relation-to' rather than 'power over'. This way, potentially, everyone in the organisation has access to being effective and powerful. When you are reading through the descriptions of the different types of power, make a

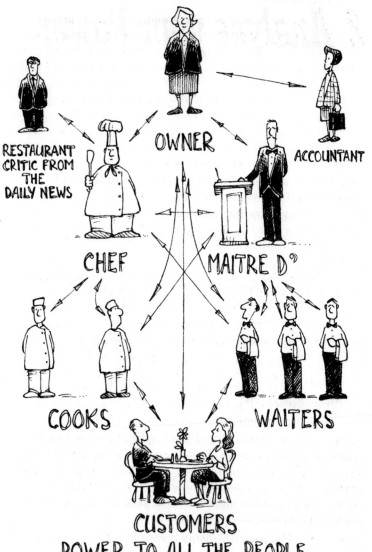

list of the ways in which you hold power in your organisation, and ask yourself if you are making the most of it.

■ *1 Formal authority*

This power is the right, through position or status, to make decisions, and is conferred on you by higher management. This formal power is seldom sufficient on its own because it depends on both seniors and subordinates accepting your right and ability to take control. Other types of power need to be used with it and it is not usually enough to metaphorically wear a badge saying, 'I'm a manager, I've got power' without some substance. This would be rather like Imposter behaviour. Even people who obviously have a high status or position prefer to use a combination of different types of power bases. The person who uses only Formal Authority is rather like the Parent who relies on the 'because I say so' method of persuasion.

- What 'formal authority' do you have?
- Who has 'formal authority' in relation to you?

■ *2 Expertise*

Specialist knowledge, skills and understanding, often acquired through professional training outside the organisation, for example, the company lawyer or accountant, is a form of power. By becoming a specialist within the organisation, for example, working in the computer department, you gain power.

- What expertise do you have?
- Could you develop any new expertise?

■ *3 Resource control*

This power is the control of physical, financial or information resources of the organisation. People in relatively low formal authority positions can have considerable resource control, for example, the switchboard operator, or the boss's secretary, the person who allocates car parking spaces. The most power however, goes to those who control the most valued resources – particularly money and information.

- What resource control do you have?
- Who has resource control in relation to you?

This power is the ability to build and develop good relationships; the ability to influence, to persuade, to communicate well, to motivate yourself and others, to delegate effectively, to negotiate fairly, to be assertive, to anticipate and tackle problems before they can damage the organisation and the people. This power not only depends on personal flair but also on acquired skills through training and practice.

- What personal skills do you have?
- What personal skills do you wish to improve upon?

The power-net

Draw a diagram of your own work power-net; follow the format of the one on the opposite page.

The people who circle YOU, are those who have an important effect on your work – they can be higher or lower than you in the hierarchy, and either inside or outside of the organisation (e.g. customers, suppliers, sub-contractors etc.) however, they have an important influence on how well you can do your job.

Power is a two-way process, so consider the following questions:

1 What types of power does each person in your net have in relation to you:

- What is their power based on?
- How are they using it?
- Why?

2 What sort of power do you have in relation to each person in your net:

- What is your power based on?
- How are you using it?
- Why?

Many of us have a combination of types of power flowing in both directions. Often, quite junior people have a strong influence and powerful role to play in a manager's ability to deliver. Look at the balance of power in different relationships. Problems can be

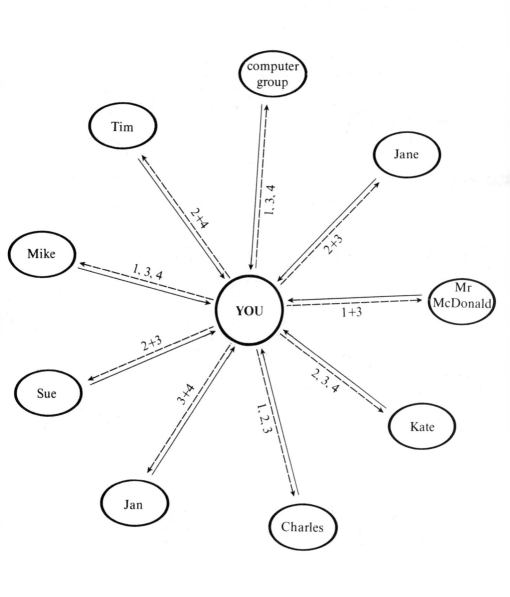

computer
group

Tim

Jane

1, 3, 4

2+4

2+3

Mike

1, 3, 4

YOU

Mr
McDonald

1+3

2+3

2, 3, 4

Sue

3+4

1, 2, 3

Kate

Jan

Charles

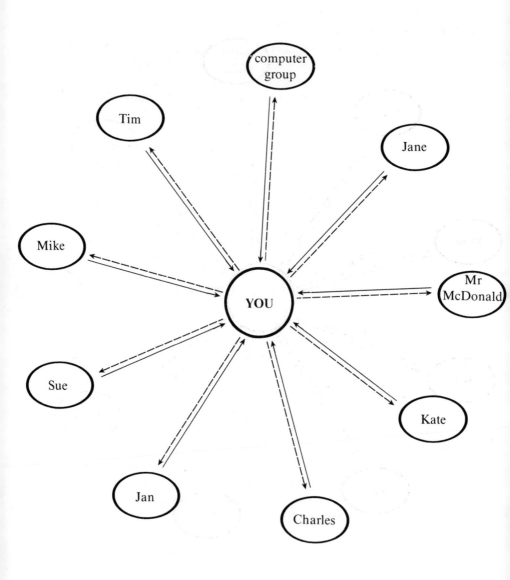

starkly highlighted when you expose an unhappy imbalance of power. (See the diagram opposite.)

Using your power-net

Use your power-net to start to change the areas you wish to improve or develop. It is very important to complete this exercise carefully because, throughout the book, the practical exercises will ask you to refer to your power-net to identify the behaviour patterns you want to change, for example:

- Are there people in your net who just don't listen to your ideas? Later on, the Broken Record technique will help you to overcome this problem.

- Are there people in your net to whom you don't listen? The Workable Compromise chapter will help you to overcome this problem.

- Are there people in your net who are very aggressive towards you; who make you feel angry or frightened? The Fogging and Inner Dialogue techniques will help you to overcome this problem.

- Use the TA table to ask yourself about the usual ego state you adopt with those people in your power-net. Are you Critical Parent, or is someone Critical Parent towards you?

Try to use the Adult mode in your next transaction with this person and compare the response you get.

- Are you always formal and 'buttoned-up' at work? Try injecting some Free Child exuberance and enthusiasm – it could work wonders.

- Are you known as the company joker – the laugh-a-minute person? Is this approach the most effective one? Are you under-valued because of it? Try to temper your Free Child with a more Adult approach.

PART THREE

1 Assertiveness Techniques

We've looked at how being assertive does not always come naturally or easily to everyone, but there are ways in which you can develop assertive skills without getting yourself in too deep, too quickly. Just as you would never expect a non-swimmer to dive in at the deep end on the first lesson, you would not expect to handle the most difficult situations or people without dipping a toe in at the shallow end to learn the basics and to see how it feels. Learning to be assertive naturally and confidently is like learning to drive a car. It can take some time and lots of practice to overcome the initial feelings of 'how does everyone else make it look so easy?' and 'there is so much to remember and co-ordinate, I'll never get the hang of this.' Just like putting an L-plate on a car, you can give yourself time and space by practising being assertive until you feel comfortable, confident and competent. Following each introduction of an assertive behaviour or skill, there will be lots of ideas for practical opportunities for you to try it out on your own or with a trusted friend or colleague and to then start to make some choices about real situations that you want to tackle without taking too much risk immediately. It is a good idea, for example, to be assertive with your milkman about the delivery times before trying out your skills with your difficult boss!

There are six different types of assertiveness and a whole range of additional techniques to help you deal with difficult or sensitive situations. In the rest of this book we will be exploring all the assertive types. They are:

- Basic Assertion
- Empathetic Assertion
- Responsive Assertion
- Discrepancy Assertion
- Negative Feelings Assertion
- Consequence Assertion

In addition we will be looking at:

- Body Language
- Workable Compromise
- Inner Dialogues
- The Broken Record
- Fogging
- Saying No (without guilt)

We're going to start by working on **Empathetic Assertion**. This assertive approach is often thought of as 'bread and butter' assertion. It is the most all-round, all-purpose type, and is particularly useful in a culture which places a high priority on valuing other people as well as yourself. In many ways the other types of assertion follow this one.

Basic Assertion is the most commonplace assertion and is used in everyday situations. It is generally used in simple, uncomplicated transactions, where you can directly state your own needs and wants. So this type of assertion is the one we use most and which we are least aware of.

Responsive Assertion involves helping silent or passive people to speak up. Sometimes their problem stems from a lack of confidence, or an inability to find the 'right words', or 'right time'. On other occasions it is strategic and the 'silent saboteur' seeks, quite deliberately, to distance themselves from the decision-making process and then they sabotage the decision or the event later. This can cause tremendous difficulties at work and Responsive Assertion helps to bring these disagreements into the open at a much earlier stage.

Discrepancy Assertion is the best way of dealing with those who give mixed messages – people who say one thing and do another. It helps to point out the inconsistency without being confrontative and can help to clear up misunderstandings before they escalate into big issues.

It is often hard to express feelings, particularly negative ones, at work. **Negative Feelings Assertion** helps you to express these feelings in a way that doesn't attribute blame. It is often better to be able to say directly how you feel, rather than show angry feelings in an indirect and indiscriminate way.

Finally, there is **Consequence Assertion,** which is the strongest form of assertion and which must be used sparingly and with a great deal of care. This type of assertion helps to point out the likely consequences of behaviour or actions in a way that does not automatically trap the other person or group into a corner.

You can see that some of these types are for very occasional use only, which is why it is especially useful to begin with Empathetic Assertion as a central starting point. Let's look at how to do it.

2 Empathetic Assertion

There are three simple steps to Empathetic Assertiveness. It is important to understand and practise all three steps as a coherent sequence – once you've mastered them, it won't feel at all mechanical and will become second nature to you.

- **Step One** – Actively listen to what is being said and then show the other person that you both hear and understand what they are saying.

- **Step Two** – Say what *you* think and feel in a direct way.

- **Step Three** – Say clearly what you want to happen.

Step One

Active listening means that you concentrate on the other person and what they are saying, or what their position is. Too often, we spend the time when another person is speaking thinking about *our* reply – our defence or attack is ready as soon as they stop talking. Most people literally pay lip-service to listening – they talk about it a lot more than they do it! By listening effectively, you can demonstrate an understanding and awareness of their views or situation even if you don't wholly agree with them. There are those who argue that the ability to listen well is the most vital management skill. In communication, it is worth remembering that we have *two* ears and only *one* mouth. Perhaps we should listen and speak in those proportions!

Step Two

Saying what you think allows you to state your own thoughts and feelings without insistence or apology. This sounds reasonable, but for some of us it can be a real struggle to say what we think or feel with confidence, and without making excuses. Very often, a 'status' or hierarchy system can inhibit us.

> *I couldn't possibly say that to them – I'm only a manager – they're executives.*

Senior people in an organisation cannot be effective if those junior to them are reluctant to give them unwelcome news. It is usually those of us who are prepared to say what we think in a calm, reasonable way who get to be in key positions, so they'll recognise it for what it is!

When you wish to present a different view, using the word 'however' is an effective way of linking Step One and Step Two. If you use the word 'but' you tend to contradict your first statement and undervalue it. 'But' can be negative and unhelpful; it is a stopping word. It is useful to think of other linking words and phrases, for example:

- on the other hand
- nevertheless
- even so
- alternatively
- in addition
- another consideration is

Step Three

This stage is about paving the forward path; an assertive person is able to present a different or alternative view and provide ideas for action or solution. This stage is essential so that you can indicate in a clear and straightforward way what action or outcome *you* want, without hesitancy or being too insistent or strident. The response you get from this approach is focused clearly on exploring solutions and not on self-defence. A good example of an everyday situation where the technique would work well is refusing a request from a person sitting next to you:

You don't mind if I have a cigarette, do you?

An aggressive response would be 'I certainly do mind. It's a disgusting habit,' or you could respond passively by saying 'Well no, I don't *really* mind,' and then cough apologetically into your handkerchief.

The assertive alternative would use the three steps:

> *I can see that you would really like a cigarette, and I appreciate you asking. I feel very uncomfortable with cigarette smoke, and I would prefer you not to.*

● *Step One* – **Actively listen to what is being said and then show the other person that you both hear and understand what they are saying.**

'I can see that you would really like another cigarette, and I appreciate you asking.'

- *Step Two* – **Say what you think and feel.**

  'I feel very uncomfortable with cigarette smoke' . . .

- *Step Three* – **Say clearly what you want to happen.**

  'I would prefer you not to.'

Once you've mastered the three steps to Empathetic Assertiveness, there are a number of key assertive behaviours and techniques which you can develop to add to your confidence and competence. Some you may need to use regularly and others much less frequently, and all are based on the belief that the three-step technique is the foundation-stone of your communication and interaction with others. They are:

- **Broken Record** – how to help you get your message across when you are not being listened to.

- **Saying No** – how to say no without aggression and without guilt.

- **Workable Compromise** – how to behave in ways which will provide good solutions to your problems.

- **Inner Dialogues** – how to influence the way you approach life by thinking in a positive, constructive way.

- **Fogging** – how to deal with aggression effectively.

- **Negative Feelings Assertion** – how to tell people when you feel upset, concerned, hurt or angry in a way which is constructive for both of you.

Empathetic assertion: Practical exercises

■ *Exercise one: Active listening*

Active listening is a skill which can be developed. It involves total concentration in order to fully understand *what* is being said and *why* it is being said. It means:

- concentrating on the *issue* being discussed

- concentrating on the *thoughts around* the issue being discussed

- concentrating on the *feelings* that are being expressed

- concentrating on *omissions* – what is not being said – the 'hidden agenda', what thoughts and feelings are being suppressed or unrecognised

- concentrating on not instantly leaping to conclusions and *suspending judgement*

You can practise active listening on your own, using a radio and cassette recorder, or a TV and video.

Choose a programme which involves people discussing personal issues, for example, an autobiographical interview and tape it.

Time yourself for three minutes listening as carefully as you can to the programme. At the end of your time, transcribe in detail everything that you can remember. Active listening will have given you some insight into the issues, thoughts, feelings and emotions expressed, as well as a recognition of any omissions. Ask yourself, 'did I come to any conclusions during the three minutes?'. If the answer is yes, ask yourself: 'was I listening accurately or was I judging?'.

Then replay the tape and check your first listening – was it as active and accurate as it might have been? Do this as often as you can, and decide what helps you to listen well.

- Do you mentally picture images?

- Do you mentally summarise the main points?

- Do you remember key words? etc.

We often have a preference for ways of communicating; we have different ways of seeing the world. Recent studies in NLP (neuro linguistic programming) have suggested that some people like to express (and identify with) ideas through one of three different senses – touch, sight or hearing, and that this can be indicated in their choice of language. Those with a preference for 'touch' or 'feeling', for example, use phrases like:

- 'Let's *take hold* of this problem and sort it out.'

- 'I think I *grasp* your meaning.'

- 'What I *feel* is going on here is . . .'

- 'Let's *toss* some ideas around.'

- 'You must *take* the bull by the horns.'
- 'In *concrete* terms it is a good deal.'
- 'Let's *put* our cards on the table.'

Others, however, are predominantly visual, and would respond with (and tune in to) 'sight' words, for example:

- 'I *see* what you are saying.'
- 'There is a *clear* way through this problem.'
- '*Focus* on the important issue.'
- 'I can't believe my *eyes*.'
- 'We *see* eye to eye on this.'
- 'A great *image* . . .'
- 'This *looks* good.'

Some of us are auditory and would express themselves using 'hearing words', for example:

- 'We need to *tune* in to customer needs.'
- 'I'm *hearing* conflicting messages from you.'
- 'I can still *hear* him saying it.'
- 'There is a lot of *static* in the department about it.'
- '*Tell* it like it is.'
- '*Sounds* good.'
- 'It's *unheard* of.'
- 'Face the *music*.'
- 'In *harmony* with you.'

The key message from these studies seems to be that it can be helpful to recognise by active listening (as one method) which way of communicating a person uses, and to match that way in any responses made.

■ *Exercise two: Practice*

Think about a situation or person you have handled recently in an unsatisfactory way, and which did not give you your desired outcome or happy ending. Analyse carefully what you did or did not do.

- Did I listen actively?
- Did I take time to let the other person know I understood what they were saying?
- Was I clear about my own thoughts and feelings?
- Did I express myself clearly?
- Did I have a clear picture of the outcome I wanted?

Now imagine yourself using the three steps to Empathetic Assertiveness. What would you say and do differently? Replay the scene mentally and try to envisage what reactions you may have had from the other person. It can sometimes help to write down your revised approach. Remember that using assertiveness can help you to buy time in a difficult situation, rather than feeling pressured to rush to an immediate and often hasty resolution.

Example:

FINANCIAL CONTROLLER	I'm looking for an 11.5 per cent increase in sales on last year in the next period, and I'm relying on you to achieve that without increasing your staffing costs. I'm sure you'll be able to manage that.
SALES MANAGER	I understand that we have to meet tight targets in the next period; what I'd like to do, however, is to look in more detail at the effect of an 11.5 per cent sales increase on the staffing before I can give a realistic response. I'd like to talk to you again after I've done that. Could we meet at about 10.30 tomorrow morning?

● ***Step One*** – **Actively listen to what is being said, and then show the other person that you both hear and understand what they are saying.**

'I understand that we have to meet tight targets in the next period.'

● ***Step Two*** – **Say what you think and feel.**

'What I'd like to do, however, is to look in more detail at the effect of an 11.5 per cent sales increase on the staffing before I can give a realistic response.'

● ***Step Three*** – **Say clearly what you want to happen.**

'I'd like to talk to you again after I've done that, how about 10.30 tomorrow morning?'

If you have a friend or colleague you feel comfortable with, brief them on the situation you've thought through, and ask them to role-play the opposite person. Measure their reactions to your assertiveness, and keep working until you feel happy with the solution you've worked out.

■ *Exercise three: Observation*

Observe and listen to a discussion/disagreement between two people (real or portrayed by actors on TV and radio) who are not being assertive – they may be being aggressive or passive, or a combination of both. Recognise where the key opportunities for assertive behaviour and solutions are being missed. Imagine or write out an alternative assertive script i.e. what might have happened had one or both parties followed the three steps. Observe and analyse your own actions, and those of others, as often as you can; decide how effective you are being, take note of what you find difficult to do, and note the areas you want to improve further. When you become confident you may well find your assertive skills will transform your life and your potential.

Reading and using the signs of Body Language

Interpreting the way that people are thinking and feeling by reading the signals they give with their bodies is not a newly discovered way of communicating, or a fashionable new training method. It is an intrinsic part of human communication – so instinctive that we sometimes don't realise what an impact our body language can have and so instinctive that we sometimes forget that we can develop and use our body language just as surely as any other communication skill.

We learn to read body language from a very early age. A baby usually smiles – only at another human face however, not at a cot mobile – at around six weeks old. It is considered such a fundamental step that it is formally charted in the baby's development records because it is recognised as the first conscious communication a human being makes. The effect, of course, can be profound and stunning. Parents who have been struggling with a relentlessly screaming bundle suddenly feel totally enslaved when 'the smile' is bestowed upon them.

Telephonists are advised to smile when on the phone because it is impossible to sound cold and distant if you are smiling. As children, we learn very quickly to recognise if someone is angry or approachable, happy or sad. Throughout our lives, our body language is often the first step in any interaction. Long before you start to speak, you are giving messages about the way you feel, for example: the manager who asks you into their office but keeps you standing waiting whilst they continue to work without looking up is saying 'you are less important than me', 'I am busy. You can wait until I have finished' and 'I have little respect for your time or feelings'.

The interviewer who makes small talk, checks journey details, talks about the weather and maintains regular, warm eye contact with some smiles is waiting for the shoulders of the interviewee to relax, for the breathing to become calm and regular and (sometimes) the deep red blush to disappear from the neckline.

It is, therefore, very important that you are giving the appropriate signals with your posture and demeanour, if your aim is to be assertive. It is not possible to be verbally assertive effectively, for example, if you don't establish regular eye contact, or if you speak in a hesitant, unsure way. You won't appear calm and in control if you hunch your shoulders and almost curl in upon yourself, in an unconscious effort to minimise your presence.

Here are some of the differences between Assertive, Aggressive and Passive body language.

Practise using assertive body language and you will find it more easy to be verbally assertive; adopting a calm, relaxed posture will help you to feel calm, relaxed and able to cope with the situation. In the most difficult situations, try stepping outside and look at your body posture – you will stop looking and sounding aggressive, for example, if you lean backwards and lower your voice tones, and you stop acting passively, for example, if you sit upright and speak firmly and evenly. There is an old proverb which says 'Lower your voices and strengthen your arguments'. Use the table on the following page to identify different sorts of body language.

Body language

	Assertive	*Aggressive*	*Passive*
Posture **Head** **Eyes**	Upright/Straight Firm not rigid. Direct not staring, good and regular eye contact.	Leaning forward. Chin jutting out. Strongly focused, staring, often piercing or glaring eye contact.	Shrinking. Head down. Glancing away, little eye contact.
Face **Voice**	Expression fits the words. Well modulated to fit content.	Set/Firm Loud/Emphatic	Smiling even when upset. Hesitant/Soft, trailing off at ends of words/ sentences.
Arms/ **Hands** **Movement/** **Walking**	Relaxed/Moving easily Measured pace suitable to action.	Controlled extreme/ sharp gestures/ fingers pointing, jabbing. Slow and heavy or fast, deliberate, hard.	Aimless/still Slow and hesitant or fast and jerky.

Body language: Practical exercises

■ *Exercise one: People-watching*

Practise 'people-watching' and interpret the signals they give – how are assertive people using their bodies? Look at people who are being aggressive – what is mirrored in their body language? Look at passive people – how do their bodies reinforce their verbal behaviour?

Particularly revealing situations can be where people are in a public place and don't know each other. Watch the person on the train who spreads over two seats deliberately to gain more room, and then watch how other people looking for a seat approach to ask if this one is free. Watch the different body language signals given to a queue jumper!

■ *Exercise two: Interpreting body language*

Videotape an interview on television but watch the scene with the volume *off*; try to interpret what is being said and how the people are feeling by reading their body language. Check how accurate you have been by replaying the tape with the volume on.

■ *Exercise three: The body language of the office*

Look at your workplace with a fresh objective eye. How do people use their offices and furniture to give signals? Are desks used as barriers or defences; is there an option to sit informally in relaxing chairs? Does everyone operate behind constantly closed doors? How do you use your office? Are you giving the signals that you want to? Your workplace is an extention of yourself – is it how you want it to be?

■ *Exercise four: You and your body language*

Using a mirror, check your usual body posture. Stand in a way in which you feel comfortable – this is probably how you usually stand. Is it an assertive posture? Sitting in an upright position, bend your head slightly to one side, and then to the other. Which side feels more comfortable to you? Be aware that the 'comfortable' position is probably the one you use when you are being passive, and trying to plead for something, or make excuses for something. Remember that a firm upright head position will help you to be assertive. Decide if you need to practise adapting your posture. Still using a mirror, practise asking a question or saying something which you would normally find difficult to do assertively. Keep practising until you find the most effective body language to reinforce your verbal skills.

■ *Exercise five: Voice control*

Practise controlling your voice-tone by reading sections of your daily newspaper aloud. Try reading the Birth and Death columns to provide you with two extremes; find a humorous article and a serious article, and try them. Find some poetry that moves you and practise reading it out loud. Write out things that you find difficult to express and practise until you find the right tones.

Be aware that the comfortable position is probably the one you use when you are being passive.

The Broken Record Technique

If at first you don't succeed, try, try again.

The Broken Record approach is about persistence, about not giving up when you meet resistance to your ideas, feelings or needs. This can happen daily in small ways as well as in larger more important ways, it is a very useful skill to develop. The technique works well with someone who isn't (or doesn't want to be) listening. Using the Broken Record will help you to persist when you get a negative or nil response; persisting, however, without anger, sarcasm, manipulation or shouting. It is not about nagging or whingeing or whining. *You simply repeat your message in a calm, thoughtful way until it gets through.*

The key part of the technique is to keep repeating your message until it is no longer ignored or dismissed – be patient and you will get there. It is important to use some of the words over and over again in different sentences. This strengthens the main part of your message and prevents others from raising red herrings or diverting you from your aims.

As an example, the following conversation illustrates the technique being used:

Production Manager to insistent customer

> We *won't be able to complete by the fifteenth.* I understand it causes you problems, but the hard facts are that it *won't be possible to complete all the work by the fifteenth.* We can promise, however, to finish key areas if you tell us your needs, and we'll reschedule the rest: *What we can't do is complete everything by the fifteenth.*

The mother of a sick child with a doctor's receptionist

MOTHER My child is ill and I would like the doctor to come to my home to examine him *this morning.*

RECEPTIONIST The doctor is holding a surgery at the moment. Why don't you bring your child in to the surgery?

MOTHER I understand that she's running a surgery; however, my child is quite ill, and I want the doctor to come and see him *this morning.*

RECEPTIONIST The doctor is already swamped with sick children who have been brought to the surgery – she's really very busy. It would be better for you to come here.

MOTHER I do realise that the doctor is very busy; nevertheless, my child is ill, and I do need the doctor to come to see him *this morning.*

RECEPTIONIST	Well . . . if you really can't come into the surgery, I'll try to fit you in after the clinic this afternoon.
MOTHER	I appreciate the suggestion, but this afternoon will be too late. My child is ill in bed, and I do feel it is necessary for him to see the doctor *this morning*.
RECEPTIONIST	Well, I'll put you on the morning visit list, but you must realise that you are at the end of a long list of urgent cases.
MOTHER	I'm glad she'll be able to come. I look forward to seeing her at some stage *this morning*. Thank you for your help.

Ray Kroc, the man who conceived of and developed the fast food company, McDonalds, has some wise words about the importance of persistence.

> *'Nothing in the world can take the place of persistence.*
> *Talent will not; nothing is more common than unsuccessful people with talent.*
> *Genius will not; unrewarded genius is almost a proverb.*
> *Education will not; the world is full of educated derelicts.*
> *Persistence and determination alone are omnipotent.'*

Broken record: Practical exercises

■ *Exercise one*

Analyse your power-nets - is there anyone who regularly does not listen to you? Anyone who never takes your ideas/suggestions on board? Practise the Broken Record technique before and during your next encounter with them.

■ *Exercise two*

Ask a friend to play the part of a very persistent salesperson, using every possible ploy to sell into your company and to get you interested in the product. You should use the Broken Record technique to get across the message that you are not interested.

■ *Exercise three*

Listen to TV and radio interviews, particularly those involving politicians, identifying when either the interviewer or politician uses the Broken Record technique to get their view across. Notice when it is used effectively, and contrast this with occasions when whining or stonewalling takes over.

3 Basic Assertion

If Empathetic Assertion is the 'bread and butter' assertion for dealing with situations where clarification and consultation is desirable, Basic Assertion is the most commonplace type of assertion used in everyday situations. It's a way of saying what you think, feel or want in a straightforward and direct way. It is generally used in simple, uncomplicated transactions when you are dealing with people in a simple, adult way. And when you feel assured that they too are able to state their feelings, thoughts or needs in a reasonable way. You can be fairly certain of a balanced, fair and equal relationship when Basic Assertion is regularly used.

■ *Examples*

- 'I think we should increase our staff.'
- 'Yesterday's meeting was not well received, I'd like to discuss it.'
- 'I feel that three days is reasonable.'
- 'Figures are not good, I believe we need to talk.'
- 'I need to set up a meeting this week.'
- 'This product looks good, I think it will be successful.'

Saying No

Saying no can prove very difficult for many of us – it can present images of truculence, selfishness, lack of sensitivity, an unwillingness to co-operate etc. Sometimes people are intimidated by the thought of an aggressive response to their no, and others need to be thought well of at all costs, for example:

Chris

'An old friend of mine has asked me to drive him and his wife to Oxford for a family wedding. I'll have to wait for them, and bring them home after the reception. It isn't a good road and it will take me over an hour each way. I really don't want to do it, but I don't want to let them down . . . and they have offered to pay for the petrol.'

What are the likely results if Chris says yes and what are the likely results if Chris says no? If Chris says yes, the friend will undoubtedly be pleased, but Chris will be angry personally for not coping in a better way with the request. The favour will not be done with good grace, the day will be miserable, and filled with increasing resentment. It is possible that these feelings might effect the relationship long-term. It will almost certainly make Chris feel cooler about the friend in the short-term.

If Chris says no, there may be some tense feelings in advance, however, overall there will be good feelings about having coped assertively with the situation. Chris' own needs will have been recognised as of equal importance as those of the friend. The friend will have to make alternative travel arrangements and will perhaps be more thoughtful about requests in the future.

There is, of course, the possibility that Chris' friend will attempt to manipulate by a withdrawal of affection, or by a display of aggression. Chris would need to be prepared to deal with these responses by remaining assertive by using the three steps of Empathetic Assertion and Broken Record technique.

Avoiding saying no can cause you bigger problems

In many situations, a reluctance to say no can lead you into greater difficulties than actually saying no. Very often, people take on more than they can cope with and then struggle, miss deadlines or produce poor quality work because they can't say no. It is much more responsible to give an initial no than to dodge the issue and then let others, and yourself, down by not coming up with the promised goods later.

In other situations you may have commitments to other people which you don't fulfil if you can't say no. This can happen when dealing with a boss – you may well have responsibility for staff whose rights or needs it is your job to represent and safeguard, for example:

Retail Store Manager to Food Supervisor

'I want all permanent store staff to start work earlier on Saturday mornings. I think if we get them in by 7.30 a.m. we can be sure of being ready for trading at 8.30 a.m. We need to get this sorted, do you agree that this is the right way to proceed?'

Food Supervisor

'No, I don't think that this is the best solution. I recognise that we need to find ways of improving our preparation for opening, nevertheless this way is not fair to the permanent staff who are already working longer hours and are under more pressure than previously. I would like to suggest we explore other ways of solving this problem.'

The food supervisor has said no, and then assertively paved the way to finding other solutions to the problem.

Saying no assertively allows you to maintain your self-respect. Often we resort to a passive no by making excuses or using what we think of as excusable lies, for example: 'I'd like to come to the conference but I can't because my mother is quite ill and I may be needed at home urgently.'

A reluctance to say no can lead you into greater difficulties.

Perhaps someone has asked to borrow your car so you give what seems a perfectly valid excuse: 'I'm really sorry, I normally would, but it is booked into the garage for service that day,' or 'I would but it's only insured for me.'

Once you've experienced the initial relief of getting out of a tight spot, you're left with a nagging feeling of unease, because it is cheating yourself to behave in such a way. It is not a good deal to lose your self-respect in order to save your face. It is, after all, perfectly reasonable to say: 'I have decided not to attend this conference,' or 'it is my rule to never lend anyone my car.' The key to an assertive no is to remember that you have the right to say it without feeling guilty or having to justify yourself.

■ Saying no – checklist

1   Assess whether the other person's request is reasonable or unreasonable. If you are hesitating or hedging, this may be a clue – *you want* to refuse.

2   Assert your right to ask for more information and clarification.

3   Practise saying no. Give a simple no – not a long-winded statement filled with excuses. A direct explanation is assertive.

4   Say no without saying 'I'm sorry, but . . .' This weakens your stand and encourages others to play on guilt feelings.

■ Saying no: Practical exercise

Use your power-nets to think about what kinds of things you find it hard to say no to and what kinds of requests and people are hard to refuse? For example, is it hard for you to refuse personal favours, social invitations, or impossible demands at work? Is it hard for you to say no to your boss, your peers, your team, your partner, your neighbour, or your children?

Make lists under the two headings 'It is hard to refuse . . .' and 'It is hard to say no to . . .'. Ask a friend to ask some tough favours of you, role-playing your difficult people and invitations. Practise saying no.

Workable Compromise: Everyone a Winner

We live and work in an era when people are more eager and prepared to become involved in decision-making and problem-solving, and less and less likely to accept decisions and solutions which have been imposed upon them. The Workable Compromise is an approach which enables people to work through problems and differences of opinion without resorting to manipulation or aggression. We all face problems, even in ordinary day-to-day situations so finding a practical solution which is acceptable to all involved abandons the winners and losers game and encourages joint winners; joint winners because each party has been listened to, has had an opportunity to say what they think and has contributed in some way to the solution.

The problems with settling for winners and losers is the difficult or unpleasant repercussions, both for the individuals and for the organisation, for example the winner may:

- listen less and less to the ideas of others.
- act aggressively in future having seen that aggression wins.
- become isolated from their colleagues as they become frightened or unwilling to take part in unpleasant exchanges.
- make decisions based on an increasingly narrow and blinkered view.

The loser may:

- stop contributing ideas through lack of confidence or resentment.
- become a silent saboteur by 'knocking' ideas and proposals in an underhand way, and without the 'protagonist' being able to deal with the objections.
- become a catalyst for disgruntled colleagues.

By using the Workable Compromise approach, you are saying it is not my solution or your solution but *our* solution.

By giving each person room to manoeuvre and to listen to each other, it is often possible to make the joint solution very much better than either of the single ones. People sometimes say when being introduced to Workable Compromise:

> 'This is wonderful in theory, but you haven't met my boss! He'd tear my head off, or laugh me out of his office saying I've gone soft.'

> 'This works fine with people that are okay, but I can't stand my counterpart in sales. No way will I ever reach a workable compromise with her.'

These feelings reflect one of the common barriers to Workable Compromise, and it regularly occurs: people address the personality not the problem.

Concentrate on the problem, not the person

Human beings have emotions which they feel committed to and which they feel strongly about; and that isn't a bad thing. Often your emotions can support Workable Compromise – if you feel committed to and trusting of the people you work and live with, you are likely to operate at a successful level in your decision-making and problem-solving. Life, however, is not always a bowl of cherries, and anger, resentment, and the feeling of being cheated or hurt can stop proceedings very quickly.

Recognise the emotions

It is a mistake not to recognise people's feelings and how you yourself are feeling. If you ignore your emotions they won't go away, but it will hinder how you approach an issue. Emotions which are running high can escalate rapidly and get out of control; one person's anger can activate anger in the other; sarcasm will provoke retaliation or withdrawal. Egos can become bruised very easily and scoring points scratches the people, not the surface of the problem. In this climate, nothing constructive can be achieved, and lots of damage can be done.

Discuss the emotions

It isn't 'soft' to discuss feelings – it is very tough for many people to admit their own feelings. By talking about how both parties are feeling, however, means that misunderstandings and concerns can be cleared up and the ground can be prepared for the way forward. This does not mean a confessional outpouring, however, it requires calm, rational communication about what is causing a block. It is reasonable to say, for example:

> *'I don't know how you are feeling. I would like to clearly establish some listening time, so that I don't end up feeling the same way again, but I am feeling uptight and resentful about this, because my ideas weren't listened to at our last meeting.'*

It is important, however, to take responsibility for your own feelings, without apportioning blame. For example, it is more constructive to say: 'I feel ignored and not listened to,' than 'You never listen to me,' or 'I felt very angry and upset during that meeeting,' rather than 'You made me very angry and upset during that meeting'.

This approach is dealt with in more detail in the Negative Feelings Assertion chapter.

Outbursts of emotion

Even if people take time and care to discuss how they are feeling, there can be times when emotions run high, and a sudden explosion can occur. If this does happen, recognise that it is letting-off steam, and don't climb on board. Be prepared to wait without responding and getting dragged in. If you do receive a full frontal attack, try to sidestep it, and concentrate on channelling the energy into solving the problem.

ATTACK	You just don't seem to have understood how much all these plans will cost – you always have your wonderful visions – but I'm the sucker who is responsible for the budget.
ASSERTIVE RESPONSE	I recognise just how committed you are to getting this problem solved; I'm equally concerned to reach a good solution. Would it be helpful for us both to take a break and write down the issues which we need to tackle?

(See the section on Fogging for more detail on how to deal with aggression.)

B language

Wher are trying to reach a mutual solution with someone, rem er to be conscious of what your posture, demeanour and v one are indicating. It is a good idea, for example, for two le working on an idea to sit side-by-side at a desk or table, rther than on opposite sides. It is usually better to stand alongside or walk with someone than to stand directly in front of them – this could be interpreted as confrontational or as an attempt at blocking. Keep your voice calm and regular and speak at a measured pace. Relax your shoulders – if you feel tense, you will act in a tense way. Be careful to be sensitive to giving just enough space; if you stand too close you can feel threatening or make the other person uneasy, and if you stand too far away, you will appear distant and cool.

Understanding viewpoints

Another fairly common reaction when discussing Workable Compromise is: 'I could never see a way in which I could reach a solution with my colleague. We don't fight, but we are always poles apart in the way we see things.'

To some people, the glass is half full, to others it is half empty. People can often have very different perceptions of the same situation or problems. Each person bases their understanding and reading of issues on a number of factors which are unique to them:

- knowledge and experience
- background
- childhood
- interests
- likes/dislikes
- values and principles

Although often the differences can contribute to effective mutual work or living, sometimes misunderstandings and misinterpretations can become real obstacles. Take, for example, the newly promoted sales manager.

Newly promoted sales manager

This manager is determined to run things differently from his predecessor, who was a very formal person; an autocratic manager. The new manager's style is deliberately open and involving. His self-perception is that he is approachable and enjoys a good laugh (after all, having a good laugh doesn't stop good work) and that he is good at encouraging people to participate fully in all aspects of work, and therefore develop themselves to their full potential. The key to this approach is flexibility, so meetings will be less formal and controlled than previously – everyone will have every opportunity to have their say and to make contributions.

Established sales staff member

'This new manager has got to be a joke. After the old boss, who was a real boss and ran a tight ship where everyone knew just what they were doing, this feels like being cast adrift without a paddle. This manager never seems to be prepared, never has a formal agenda at meetings, and doesn't take control. Leadership has gone out of the window – this is chaos. This is a weak boss, and my best bet is to stand well back and watch the fiasco develop; he won't last long.'

This polarisation of perceptions could lead to disaster, but it needn't if the two parties follow some simple guidelines.

■ *Sit in the other seat*

It always helps to try to see the situation from the other person's position; 'walk a mile in their shoes' is a good motto to remember. If the new manager put themselves in their sales staffs' shoes, they might ask themselves:

- How did I feel when I had a new boss who was completely different from the previous one?

- What makes this person tick: when do they work best, what are their strengths, what makes them feel threatened, what makes them feel angry, what are their weak points?

- How can I support and encourage them to achieve even better sales? What are they looking for in a good boss?

- What am I doing now that is hindering them? Will confronting them at the next meeting work well?

The sales staff might ask themselves:

- When I took over my role, did I want to be judged immediately by my subordinates? What effect would that have had on me?

- How long did it take me to settle down and understand my job, and then perform at a consistently high level?

- How do I feel when one of my subordinates does not participate fully? What do I think about them?

- What do they want from me? What do they look for in a good salesperson?

This approach can provide lots of 'hooks and eyes' for people working together rather than each person sticking resolutely to their own path.

Be flexible

It is very important to allow space for people to be able to change their position or alter their course, without losing their own self-respect and the respect of others. If the sales manager feels that the sales staff has undermined him/her in the department by playing the silent saboteur, they may well fight their corner at all costs in order to demonstrate that they're not a push-over. 'Relaxed, maybe, soft – never.'

If, on the other hand, the sales executive is confronted about their concerns in front of their colleagues at a meeting, they may well feel their only response can be aggression and may come out with a tirade of criticisms of the new manager's leadership style. 'If I go down, I'll go down fighting.'

If, however, both parties recognise the feelings and perception of the other, they are more likely to approach working together in a logical, positive way, exploring ways to reach their shared goal – to achieve higher sales figures. They may never be bosom pals, but they might be able to pitch tents in the same field!

Concentrate on the desired outcome

Too often, people do back themselves, or allow themselves to be backed by others, into a corner. It helps to look at the reasons for the stated positions, rather than simply attack or defend it.

■ *Example*

HUSBAND: I want to have our summer holiday in France.
WIFE: I want to have our summer holiday in Yorkshire.

The two positions appear unmatchable, but when the reasons for them emerge, areas for compromise also emerge.

HUSBAND: I particularly want to go to France to visit the D-day landing beaches and the war museums in the fortieth anniversary year of Dunkirk.

WIFE: I want to go to Yorkshire to have a seaside holiday with the children and my parents.

Possible solution

Husband, wife and children and parents go to France. The wife has her seaside holiday and the husband sees the D-day beaches.

■ *Example*

MANAGING DIRECTOR: I want to sell the business. I've got a buyer who can't guarantee any jobs, so you might be made redundant.

EMPLOYEES: We refuse to move out. We'll occupy the building.

Workable compromise

In discussions, it emerges that the owner doesn't really want to sell until a bit nearer retirement but there is a buyer now. The workers have built the business with their skill and expertise and want it to continue. The boss gives the employees a chance to explore a management buy-out, or workers collective. The owner gets the retirement money and they keep the business and their jobs. Even if they can't achieve a buy-out in the final analysis, the workers feel they have been properly considered and given a fair chance.

Look forward not backward

When people have a disagreement or conflict there is always the risk of opening old wounds and revisiting past battle grounds:

> *'If you had not agreed to give merit increases last year, we wouldn't be faced with such an outrageous wage demand this year. You simply raised expectations to an unrealistic level.'*

Always channel the energy into solving the current problem well. An assertive response to this attack might be:

> *'I recognise that you didn't agree with the merit increase, I feel however, that we need to look at this year's negotiations in detail before making any new decisions and I'd like to concentrate on that in this meeting.'*

Be firm

It is important to be flexible; nevertheless, it is also important to be firm. You need to know what you want, what you believe to be right and how you want it to happen, while still being open to new ideas and fresh approaches. Don't be afraid to display your strength of conviction about the problem. Be considerate, sensitive and thoughtful to the person – save the attack for the problem. For example, if in negotiation with the Finance Manager about the cost of a project to remove asbestos from the building you might argue as follows:

> *'I understand that we have to give serious consideration to our budgets, I don't believe, however, that you want to give higher priority to cutting costs than to eliminating possible health risks to our staff. I really believe that we should look at other ways to control our budget over the next year but that we should continue to show maximum concern to the well-being of our employees. Cost cutting in this area is a false economy.'*

Use the experts

In some situations, however, if you decide to try for a workable compromise by basing your arguments purely on will or personal belief, you may well come unstuck. It can be particularly helpful to have solid objective information and facts which have been provided by an independent, objective third party. For example, during a house purchase the following situation may occur.

■ *Example I*

The sellers believe their house to be worth £150 000 and the buyer believes it is worth no more than £132 000. Each have said they are prepared to bend by no more than £5000, leaving an £8000 gap. The independent survey however, values the house at £142 000 and estimates that it needs to have approximately £2500 spent on rewiring. Both parties are more likely to find it acceptable to work towards a solution using the independent figures. Each will feel reassured that they are getting the best price possible, rather than feeling that they are getting a bad deal.

■ *Example II*

City Councillors believe and have firmly stated that they need an annual budget of £2½ million, to provide the refuse collection service for this City. There are no possibilities of economies here. They believe they are operating to the optimum efficiency.

The City Treasurers responded to this by saying that it could be helpful to look further at the budget of Barchester City Council, who are under very similar circumstances, provide services at the same level, to the same number of people for £2 million. If we compare our detailed break-down of budget, we may well find some indications for improved efficiency and economy.'

Explore all the options

All too often, people neglect to explore all the options in their eagerness to win their corner. The classic example is of two chefs who each needed six eggs, with only six eggs left in the kitchen. They decided reluctantly to compromise and have three each, each feeling that it was the only, but poor solution. One chef then used the egg whites to make the meringues and threw away the yolks, the other used the yolks to make mayonnaise and discarded the whites. If every option had been properly explored, one chef could have had six whites and the other had the six yolks. In some instances, all the options are not considered because of a reluctance of some people to become involved and it is then that Responsive Assertion can be used effectively.

4 Responsive Assertion

There are two different circumstances where Responsive Assertion can be particularly useful. Both involve getting silent or passive people to speak up and respond.

Sometimes quiet or passive people appear to be silent observers of life with little or no involvement in the happenings around them. It can be important to check their understanding or seek their views without putting them on the spot. Sometimes, this silence stems from a lack of confidence or a difficulty in finding the 'right' words or even the 'right' time to say them. Responsive Assertion enables you to find out their views and helps them to have access to the 'right time'.

Of course, there are times when passivity is used strategically to allow people to keep their heads down when a decision is being taken or a difficult issue is being discussed and then speak up in a negative way in private or disassociate themselves from events afterwards. These 'silent saboteurs' can be very unproductive working colleagues and very difficult to deal with. Once again Responsive Assertion can help to clarify these situations early and deal with lack of support and disagreements in an open and non-confrontational way.

When you use Responsive Assertion it is important to remember that you are trying to encourage others to respond in order to be clear about their views, feelings or thoughts and you are *not* doing it to catch them unawares.

Example of Responsive Assertion

'So far we have heard from both production and marketing about how the new guidelines will affect them, Chris, I'd like to ask you to give us your views about how they will affect staffing.'

'We've discussed the new appointment at some length now and there seems to be broad agreement that the external candidate is the most apropriate choice. Before we make a final decision it's important to be clear about the support this decision can expect. I'd like to start with you, Chris, what do you think?'

Creative thinking – encouraging responsiveness

Thinking creatively is the ability to use all our skills, aptitudes and attitudes to solve problems and to reach decisions. This can be hard because of what is expected in work or in professional situations. Sometimes, for example, an idea produced by someone fooling around, or having a wild thought, will be shot down before it even has a chance to be heard. It is interesting to look at some of the research that has been done on creative thinking and the physiological structure of the brain which determines our thinking and our behaviour.

Roger Sperry, an American brain surgeon, received a Nobel prize in 1981 for his research on the right and left brain hemispheres. These two hemispheres enable us to use two very different approaches to problem-solving. Typically, the left side of the brain is the part that specialises in rational, logical, analytical patterns. It is the planning and organising part of the brain. In lay terms, the left side of the brain is your built-in Filofax. The right side of the brain, on the other hand, is the part where intuitive thinking and conceptualising occurs. The right hemisphere is the area where musical appreciation and our emotional thinking occurs. The right hemisphere of the brain helps us to see the whole problem, whereas the left side is the detailed-planning centre.

Our right-brain/left-brain preferences are as unique as our thumb prints and they determine the way in which we like to approach problem-solving and decision-making. Have a look at the lists of adjectives and descriptions below and try to decide which fits you best.

Left-brain	Right-brain
Logical, rational	Creative
A good adminstrator	Innovative
Organised	Intuitive
Need for detail	Emotional
Controlled	Artistic
Analytical	Talkative
Technical	Spiritual
Likes to get down to the 'nitty gritty'	Likes to see the whole picture
	Likes to work on a broad based structure

Clearly, there are some people who are very successful at using both hemispheres, but more often most of us do have a leaning towards one or other pattern of thinking. Some of our jobs require us to concentrate on using one hemisphere more than the other. The left-brain professionals, for example, are lawyers, accountants, bankers, engineers, town planners, administrators etc. Whereas the right-brain professionals are nurses, writers, teachers, artists, musicians, probation officers and social workers etc.

Problem-solving in a team can work well when there is a good mix of people together using both right-brain and left-brain thinking and who are prepared to combine the best of their skills. Problems are then approached from all angles, with uninhibited vision and with appropriate consideration and concern for the people involved. It was, for example, a right-brain thinker who said: 'Let's put a man on the moon', and a left-brain thinker who said: 'In order to get a man on the moon we need a ten-year programme, with clearly defined targets.' One of the best ways of exploring all of the options is to use a simple brainstorming technique. This is a way of creating and capturing ideas without judging them or looking for the problems straightaway. Let anyone and everyone float their ideas without fear of ridicule or criticism and you might just come up with the winning answer, or, at least, the beginning of an answer. To get this we need to allow the 'creative leap' – the bright idea – to happen. Think of the criticism and jeers the following bright ideas must have encountered.

When banking hours limited customer use and staffing costs made longer hours an unacceptable solution, someone had the bright idea of knocking a hole in the wall of the bank and letting customers just come in and take the money whenever they wanted it, and so cash-points were born!

At one time, customers in all shops were served individually by staff, then someone said, 'Why don't we just let them help themselves?', and so we now have supermarkets.

When you are brainstorming, avoid writing lists as that can indicate priorities and order of importance. Simply write the problem in the middle of the page and note down all the options and suggestions in a circle around the centre, as they occur.

Workable compromise checklist

- Look for win/win solution
- Concentrate on the problem not the personality
- Recognise and discuss blocking emotions
- Encourage responsiveness
- Be aware of your posture and voice tones
- Walk a mile in their shoes
- Be flexible, but firm in your beliefs
- Use the experts wisely
- Concentrate on the desired outcome
- Look forward not backward
- Explore all the options

Workable Compromise: Practical exercise

How to develop your workable compromise approach

Identify – at work, in your personal life, and as an observer of local/national/world politics – situations that seem unworkable and where there is no movement between two solutions. Brainstorm until you arrive at real alternatives.

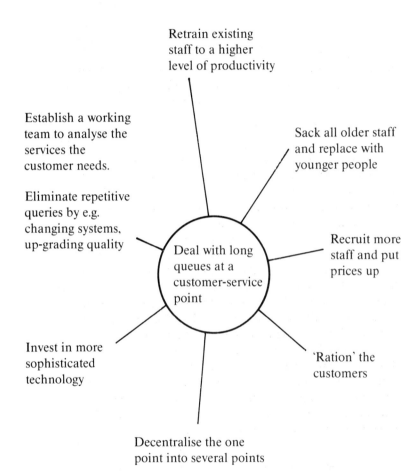

Retrain existing staff to a higher level of productivity

Establish a working team to analyse the services the customer needs.

Eliminate repetitive queries by e.g. changing systems, up-grading quality

Sack all older staff and replace with younger people

Deal with long queues at a customer-service point

Recruit more staff and put prices up

Invest in more sophisticated technology

'Ration' the customers

Decentralise the one point into several points

Inner Dialogues: Positive Thinking

How many times have you said to yourself, 'I can't do this' or 'This is going to be awful, I'm dreading it and I know it's going to go wrong'. People can often become paralysed by thinking ahead and stripping themselves of self-confidence and balance. This negative, downward spiral of thought very often ends in self-fulfilling disasters, which will then influence the way we approach our next problem, and so the spiral continues:

> 'Whether you think you can, or you can't, you're probably right'
> Henry Ford

This Negative Inner Dialogue can sometimes result in our not getting involved in discussions or situations at all. How many times have you talked yourself out of an idea saying, 'Well, it probably wouldn't work anyway', or stopped yourself from contributing to a discussion because you convinced yourself you had nothing of value to add. The 'you can if you think you can' approach has been successfully adopted by sports coaches throughout the world and there are now lots of books about the Inner Dialogue games of tennis, golf, squash, football and other sports. It is universally recognised that having a positive frame of mind and the will to win, can materially affect the way a player performs. You sometimes hear, for example, young players who perform superbly at Wimbledon on an outer court, say how the thought of appearing on the Centre Court had damaged their ability to play at their best and they give a miserable lacklustre performance. Similarly, a manager approaching a meeting with a senior executive can easily mould their performance with an Inner Dialogue which might go like this:

> 'I haven't had enough experience . . . this manager is the best in the business. I made that stupid mistake last week that cost us so much money – every time I think about it I want to curl up and die. I'll probaby be asked things that I ought to know, I know I won't know them. My throat feels so dry I won't be able to speak anyway. I wish I was off ill today, anywhere but here . . .'

At every level of management it's easy to talk yourself into a negative frame of mind; experienced managers can disable themselves just as effectively as newcomers to the technique!

'It's Friday, the budget meeting is today, it's a difficult enough meeting at the best of times and today I'm going to have to ask for extra cash, it won't go down well . . .

They'll tell me I didn't do my forward planning well enough. It's not my fault, I didn't know what would happen to prices. But they won't accept that . . .

This is just the chance admin have been waiting for, now they'll have a go at me about expenses in general. I know I won't get the extra money. It's not all one-sided, though, admin have been sending out duff information, and too late. The best form of defence is attack, I'll get in and have a go first. And another thing I can get them on is the temp they didn't send me. I can't wait to get started. I won't get the money, but I won't go down without a fight.'

Just as sports people can measurably improve their performance by thinking positively, so can the rest of us. The Positive Inner Dialogue technique is good to use when you're facing a demanding or tricky situation and want to coach yourself into doing your best. Thinking positively is not about adopting the ostrich approach and ignoring any potential problems; it is a way of stopping the downward spiral by recognising that whatever you're facing is going to be tough; however, you've prepared as well as you can for it, and you can now give it your very best. For example, the manager facing an encounter with the senior executive might say to themselves in a Positive Inner Dialogue:

'I'm learning all the time and I've come a long way since I joined this business . . . I've made some mistakes but I've also had some real successes. After all, the new ordering system I devised is working really well. I won't be expected to know everything and it is a good opportunity for me to learn more from them. I do feel nervous, but that isn't a bad thing, I often perform better when my adrenalin is flowing.'

A more experienced manager could approach the meeting in a more positive, realistic way by saying:

'It's Friday, the budget meeting is today. It's not going to be an easy meeting as I'm going to ask for extra money. I do have a good case and I can demonstrate that it's valid. Not everyone will be helpful. If there's any game playing I won't get hooked in. I do know how to be assertive and I believe I can present my case well. I'll do my best to see my department has a fair hearing. Now, what else is happening today?'

Using Positive Inner Dialogue helps you not to be trapped by your anxiety but motivated by it. If you can channel the energy you are using worrying about the situation into planning how to approach it effectively, you will be creating opportunities rather than running away from imagined hazards. It can help to think about your own strengths and your past successes when approaching a demanding situation. We often dwell upon our mistakes and weaknesses when we feel defensive and vulnerable. Self-belief is vital to your performance, so devote some time to building up your own positive personal profile so that you can feel confident when facing difficulties. Self-belief can survive failure and success, triumphs and mistakes, acceptance and rejection. A personal profile might look like this:

- I can think on my feet, so I'm not afraid of facing tricky situations.
- I've dealt assertively with aggressive managers and even if I haven't always won the case, I've been happy with the way I've performed.
- I have made mistakes but that's okay, I'm a human being.
- My strength is that I learn from my mistakes, I never make the same one twice.
- Although I used to be passive when dealing with difficult appraisal interviews, I've learnt a lot from the mistakes I made then and I am now much better able to deal with this appraisal.

In many cultures, managers can be excellent at listing their own weaknesses and areas for improvement. This is often a healthy approach, however, it does need to be counterbalanced by the ability to recognise and use their strengths and successes and so build and develop them. The Winning Circle, which is based on transactional analysis is a useful indicator of the types of images people have about themselves and about others, and how that can affect their behaviour.

The winning circle

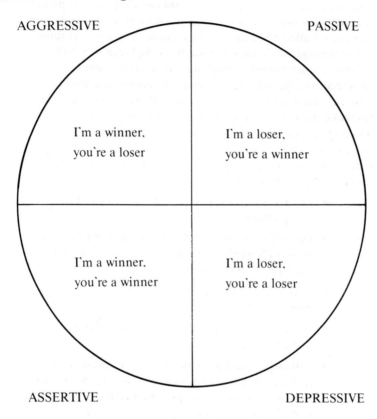

AGGRESSIVE ... PASSIVE

I'm a winner,
you're a loser

I'm a loser,
you're a winner

I'm a winner,
you're a winner

I'm a loser,
you're a loser

ASSERTIVE ... DEPRESSIVE

I'm a winner, you're a loser:

An aggressive person has a self-image that says: 'Where I am and what I'm doing and where I come from is fine – the problem is with the rest of the world.'

This self-image leads to a lack of care and respect for other people and their feelings: 'It doesn't matter what effect my behaviour has upon you because the important thing here is that I'm fine and I intend to stay fine come what may and at whatever cost to others. If you can't look out for yourself then you're not fine and it's your problem.'

This image can also have an impact on the way an individual works within an organisation. It can lead to the classic, 'it wasn't me, it was him', mentality, a refusal to take responsibility for your own actions and behaviour by blaming someone or something else, for example: 'It's not up to me, it's company policy. I don't agree with it but there it is, policy is policy', and 'It's not my fault you're tickets didn't arrive, that damn computer is playing up again', and 'If you'd done your job properly this mess would never have happened. This is your problem sunshine'.

I'm a loser, you're a winner

People who display passive behaviour often have a self-image that is poor, in contrast to everyone else around them, who seem always to perform much better than they can. Sometimes their self-perception of being a failure is used to excuse themselves from tackling issues or situations that threaten them, for example: 'I'm absolutely useless with computers, I'd rather not get involved. I'd rather just stay as I am, if that's okay with you', or 'I've never been asked to do this before. I know I'll get it wrong. I simply won't be able to do this at all.'

Because they never allow themselves to rise to a challenge or to achieve some success, this passive mode is reinforced: 'I am still losing and everyone else is winning even more.' In other circumstances, the passive person will fall over themselves to take the blame, to apologise profusely and then spend hours punishing themselves for mistakes which are fairly minor – a real Critical Parent stance. Every little mishap becomes larger than life and further proof of inadequacy and so the passive cycle continues.

The impact a passive loser can have on an organisation can be very damaging. They can:

- stunt the creativity of others through their anxiety.
- dampen activity through their negative approach.
- be afraid to speak out and therefore exacerbate rather than prevent and solve problems.
- divert attention from issues onto their personality through constant 'confessions' and 'apologies'.

I'm a loser, you're a loser

The self-image of the double-edged loser is: 'I'm a loser because everything I do goes wrong, everything I've ever been involved in has always gone wrong and the future is more of the same.' This devastating self-image leads to one of two (and sometimes both) types of behaviour – depressive or aggressive. The depressive loser behaves towards others in a negative, condemning way because 'you're part of this system where everything is wrong, and you do nothing to change it or to help me. I hold you responsible for things going wrong, in some ways.'

Depressives at work often invite condemnation by, for example:

- consistently producing poor quality work
- consistently missing deadlines, production targets, meetings etc
- violating company policies or procedures
- drinking excessively or abusing drugs

The inevitable kick simply reinforces the view that they are awful and that the world is awful.

Aggressive losers behave to others in a disruptive, angry way and refuse to accept responsibility for their own behaviour and actions. Verbal violence and bitter, open attacks on both other people's personalities and contributions typify the difficulties for an organisation that an aggressive loser creates.

> *'This section leader is an idiot. The department is so badly run, how can I get my work right?'*

> *'The personnel philosophy of this company is a pack of lies. I've done ten years and what bloody promotion has come my way? It's not what you know, it's who you know in this corruption-ridden outfit.'*

I'm a winner, you're a winner

Assertive people have a confident, positive self-image:

> *'What I am doing and where I want to go is fine, and it's also important to me that what you are doing and where you are going is fine for you. How can we work together to make sure that this is how it happens?'*

A no-win situation – I'm a loser, you're a loser.

As a result, their behaviour is constructive and positive. An assertive person doesn't play games around 'everything will be fine except for the company policy'. If there is a problem, it is dealt with in a thoughtful and balanced way. Being assertive, they accept responsibility, both for changing things and for mistakes that can occur. Assertive people allow for mistakes without self-castigation, because mistakes are human, can be put right, can be learnt from, and should be looked at in perspective. They also allow for others to make mistakes without rubbing their noses in it: 'the same rules that apply for me, also apply equally for you.'

I'm a winner, you're a winner behaviour allows for risks to be taken and demanding challenges to be met. The self-confidence born of responding well to challenges, coping with and learning from either the success or the failure, is a springboard for further jumps into new, exciting or difficult situations.

Positive inner dialogue: Practical exercises

■ *Exercise one*

Get what is in, out. It is amazing how effective it can be to voice your own fears. Have a dialogue with yourself or with a trusted friend or colleague when you recognise that your inner thoughts are leading you into an anxiety trap.

OUTER   What is it that's making you feel so anxious?

INNER   I'm concerned about the presentation I'm going to give to the executive meeting tomorrow, I'm sure it's going to be a disaster.

OUTER   Why is it going to be a disaster, haven't you done any work for it?

INNER   Yes, I've worked for hours on it, I'm just so nervous I know I'm going to blow it.

OUTER   Well, if you've worked for hours on it you must be satisfied with the material that you've prepared.

INNER   Oh, yes, it isn't the material, it's the thought of having to stand up and talk to these people, it's just terrifying.

OUTER   Right, the material is good so it's just getting over the nerves. I thought you knew these people.

INNER   Yes, I've met them individually and that was fine, but in a group – that's a different matter.

OUTER   So, you know that these people are reasonable and that they will want to hear what you've got to say.

INNER   Yes, that is true, but I've got all the technical details to handle as well and I'm useless on technical details . . . I've got to do the video and the overhead projector . . . I've got to get all the timings right . . .

OUTER   Okay, so today you can run through all the technical details to iron out any wrinkles before tomorrow. You'll then be well prepared and ready for anything. You know you're good at handling problems or questions off the cuff, so look at it as an opportunity to really perform well and get your message across effectively.

■ *Exercise two*

It can sometimes help to put yourself through the worst case test. This helps to put your anticipated problem into perspective.

INNER   I know this presentation is going to be a disaster, I'd do anything not to be here.

OUTER   Okay, so even if it is a disaster, what is the worst thing that could happen to you as a result?

INNER   Well, it could be the ruin of me.

OUTER   How would it be the ruin of you?

INNER   I could be fired.

OUTER   How likely is it that you're going to be fired? When was the last time that someone was fired for a bad presentation?

INNER   Well, I don't know . . .

OUTER   Even if you are fired is that the end of your world? Is this the only job you could ever do?

INNER   No, but my whole career would be finished.

OUTER   Why would it be finished? You've always said you'd like to do something completely different.

INNER   Yes, but I want to be a success in this job, not a failure.

OUTER   Fine, so concentrate on your successes and stop worrying about possible failures – go for it! The worst is not nearly as bad as you imagine it is.

The Fogging Technique

Fogging is a technique which can help you deal with aggression by disarming the aggressor. Aggressors expect to be met either by returned aggression or by defensiveness. Either approach can add fuel to their fire and give them more ammunition. By fogging you can side-step the aggression without becoming involved and without abandoning your position. It is a refusal to take up arms but without backing down and losing self-respect. The fogging technique enables you to recognise what is happening without agreeing with it. So, for example, if someone attacks you unreasonably by saying: 'Well you let your feelings overrule your logic in that meeting, you were very immature'. You might respond with fogging by saying: 'Yes, I recognise that you feel I was being immature'.

Using a positive yes without agreeing with the assertion that you were being immature can stop the attack effectively. The technique is called 'fogging' because it acts like a blanket of fog dropping suddenly; it is the unexpected. It is hard to see through or round and so it slows up those who encounter it. It's the verbal equivalent of standing alongside someone rather than standing head-on or face-to-face with them. It's very useful when dealing with explosions of anger without putting your own boxing gloves on. It can help you to steer the situation away from the anger, towards calm and rational discussion. For example, an irate manager might say, 'You have absolutely no mandate to discuss this with the departmental managers, this is my decision and I will not have it discussed with them.'

An assertive assistant manager might reply, 'Yes, I can see that you want no further discussion, I'd like to try and tackle the situation tomorrow when we've both had a chance to look at the issues again.'

Example

NEWLY REDUNDANT MANAGER	I can't believe that this bloody company has let me down. They won't be able to manage without me.

| PERSONNEL MANAGER (FOGGING) | Yes, I know that it must be a shock and that you feel that the company has let you down and you do have valuable knowledge and experience. Let's look at the possibilities which would be best for all. |

This example illustrates the best use of fogging; to call a halt to the aggression and anger, and to direct the discussion forward in a positive way – towards a Workable Compromise. Assertive body language is helpful here – maintaining regular eye contact effectively reinforces your verbal assertiveness. Be aware of your voice tone – keep it regular and calm – clipped, cold tones will give the impression of suppressed anger and a wavering, unsteady voice will indicate that you are thrown off-balance or overwhelmed by the attack.

Fogging is a good way of buying time when you are faced with an outburst of emotion; it can allow for the bubble to burst and a calming period to follow.

Fogging: Practical exercises

■ *Exercise one*

- Look at your power-net.

- Is there someone who regularly deals with problems by attacking you?

- What invalid criticisms do they make of you?

- Practise retrospective Fogging – how else could you have replied?

■ *Exercise two*

Make two lists for yourself – one of criticisms of yourself which are valid, one of criticisms which are not. Ask a friend to give you feedback from both lists in an aggressive way – this will help you practise making choices about fogging – whether you use it to simply calm down the situation and remain uninvolved, or whether you need to use it to pave the way towards Workable Compromise. Either way, you need to deal with it.

INSULT	FOG
'I can't believe you chose that outfit! The colour is all wrong.'	'Yes, taste is such a personal thing, isn't it?'
'How come your office always looks like a disaster area?'	'Yes, isn't it interesting how people work differently?'

5 Negative Feelings Assertion

In the earlier chapter on Workable Compromise, we looked at how people often find it difficult to express directly how they're feeling, especially in a work environment. It is often particularly difficult to express feelings which are negative. To say that you are unhappy about a situation is clearly more difficult than to say that you are happy about a situation. People often tend to swallow their feelings with a view that there is no sentiment in business. It's really impossible however, to operate effectively if you're feeling hurt, undervalued, angry, vulnerable, or used. You cannot swallow the feelings without swallowing the resentment which will stay with you and affect your self-image and your performance. Equally, blowing up might satisfy you initially, but the long-term effect of losing your self-control and self-respect can be damaging.

An assertive way to deal with negative feelings is to *express them in a way which doesn't attribute blame but which does acknowledge and recognise the importance of those feelings.* It allows for you to point out clearly what is happening, how you feel about it and what you would like to happen, for example:

> *'Yes, I can see that you are very angry and I agree that we need to discuss this matter urgently. When you shout at me in front of my colleagues however, I feel embarrassed and I feel angry. When I feel like this I can't concentrate on the issues, so I would prefer that we continue this discussion in private and without raised voices.'*

Negative Feelings Assertion has four stages. In the first, you isolate the *behaviour* or *action* which you feel strongly about. Second, you point out the *effect* this has. Thirdly, you tell them directly what *feelings* you have about this and finally you say what you *want to happen.* Another example:

> *'Each time you arrive at the meeting unprepared it means that we have to recap for your benefit only. I feel irritated about this and in future I would ask you to prepare in advance.'*

BEHAVIOUR   1   'Each time you arrive at the meeting unprepared it means . . .

EFFECT   2   that we have to recap for your benefit only.

FEELINGS   3   I feel irritated about this and in the future

ACTION   4   I would ask you to prepare in advance.'

Dealing with criticism

Dealing with criticism whether giving it or receiving it, is often cited by managers as one of the most difficult things they face. Assertive managers use criticism in a positive and constructive way and are able to give calm and rational thought to both the problem and to possible solutions. They would take pains to be objective and to be clear about the actions and behaviours which needed to be changed. They would not, for example, make subjective criticisms of personality,

> *'You have an amazing knack of putting people's backs up by saying the wrong thing at the wrong time, you just open your mouth and put your foot in it.'*

The criticism would be clear, positive and constructive,

> *'I believe you could improve the timing of some of your contributions at meetings. At our last departmental meeting, for example, it was unhelpful to insist on a discussion about individual responsibilities when so many people are still getting to grips with their new roles. What do you think? How can we work together to help you overcome this difficulty? I suggest that we start by . . .'*

Not all criticism, however, is given assertively. Aggressive criticism can be momentarily stunning and the more typical form of veiled sarcasm, or semi-humorous put-downs can be extremely hard to handle.

Handling criticism assertively

This means deciding how you are going to handle the criticism by making some assessments about it. You can ask yourself,

1 Is this criticism, or any part of it, valid and therefore useful to me?
2 How do I feel about how the criticism is being given to me?
3 How am I going to use the criticism?

If you decide that the criticism, or some part of it, is valid and that it has been given assertively, you acknowledge that it's true and ask for more specific information if you need it. You will need to decide whether you are going to change your behaviour and how you plan to do that. Don't be afraid to ask for help. It is a sign of strength, not weakness, for example, a manager on being told that their administration skills were below standard:

> *'I hadn't consciously recognised that I am slow at handling the administration part of my job, but it is the part that I feel most uncomfortable with, so that's a good indicator that my pace isn't what it should be. I would like to improve as I'm keen to do well in this job. My initial thoughts are that I will need to set some specific targets for achieving better results. Do you have any ideas that could help me? I could do some further training, or perhaps be attached to someone with more experience.'*

If, however, you decide that the criticism is valid but has been given in a way which makes you feel angry or upset, your assertive response needs to deal with both the criticism and your feelings.

The criticism

> *'I'm furious about this report. It is appalling, there are some basic errors in it, it's obvious it hasn't been checked. This is just typical of your sloppy approach.'*

> *'Yes, I can see that the report needs further work. However, when you take this report and then generalise it to all my work it could affect my appraisal. I feel disappointed and angry that you can make such a general criticism based on one report. I'd like time to look further at this report and then discuss it with you as well as my general performance.'*

This response initially uses Fogging to stop the flow of aggression, leading to a recognition of the truth of the criticism and an acceptance of responsibility for the mistake. The Negative Feelings Assertion then allows for a calm, clear rejection of the invalid criticism and an expression of the feelings that it has engendered. The recipient can now deal with the criticism without feeling angry and resentful and without having swallowed their self-respect.

6 Discrepancy Assertion

Discrepancy Assertion is used in situations where you are receiving contradictory messages. In a fast paced, fast changing work scenario, contradictory messages are one of the by-products. It is important to be able to be clear about what is actually happening or expected without using guesswork. Discrepancy Assertion helps to clear up misunderstandings before they grow into difficult issues. It is also a useful way to point out to someone the inconsistency in their behaviour without blaming or being accusatory and it helps to move people nearer to a Workable Compromise. With Discrepancy Assertion it is important to be as objective as possible pointing out the known facts clearly.

Example

> *'Earlier this month we agreed that I would be given additional resources to manage the end of the month figures. Today, I got a memo from you saying we had to cut back on staff numbers. I'd like to be clear about how this affects our first agreement.'*

OR

> *'At my staff appraisal we both agreed I was taking on too much work and it was causing me a lot of stress. In the last few weeks my department has been given several additional new projects. I'd like to discuss the implications of this extra work.'*

Using Assertiveness for Effective Appraisals

Giving and receiving criticism in a constructive and thoughtful way is an essential requisite for effective appraisal systems within a company: very often, appraisals skim over the surface of poor performances and highlight only the positive areas because we are hesitant about dealing with uncomfortable issues – and that works both ways. It is just as hard for the person receiving the appraisal to tackle a discussion of their concerns, as for the person giving the appraisal to highlight areas of weakness. As a result, appraisals can become a mechanical process with little meaning, to the detriment of both the organisation and the individual.

Using assertiveness skills in the appraisal process ensures that all the issues can be tackled fairly and reasonably.

■ Empathetic assertion

Step One

Listen actively to what is being said, and show that you hear and understand.
Both the appraiser and appraisee are thus able to fully understand the other's thoughts and views of the individual's performance, and therefore do not approach the appraisal in an inflexible or rigid frame of mind.

Step Two

Say what you think and feel
Both parties have an opportunity to discuss the issues and are more likely to have prepared thoroughly for this part of the appraisal, rather than waiting to react to ill-prepared, unsubstantiated and subjective statements.

Step Three

Say clearly what you want to happen
The appraisal is given impetus and direction, as both parties will have a clear understanding of what action needs to be taken and how that is going to happen. Even appraisals that are fulsome are negative if no developmental action is agreed.

People on the receiving end of the 'pat-on-the-back-just-do-more-of-the-same' appraisal often respond with a 'so what', and become discontented and feel undervalued, or vote with their feet and move to a more developmental department or organisation. An assertive appraisal process ensures that both parties can clearly contribute to decisions about the future – both for the individual and for the organisation.

The assertive appraisal process

Checklist

- Plan thoroughly for the appraisal – give yourself enough time to think about what you want to say.
- Listen carefully and be responsive.
- Be objective.
- Concentrate on actions and behaviour, not personality.
- Be prepared to adapt your views. However, also be prepared to be firm.
- Decide what you want to achieve; reach agreement on future action and development.
- Set realistic targets and agree a time schedule for them.

Practical exercises

1   Look at your work power-net. Who appraises you? What is your relationship with that person? Are you happy with the way you communicate? If not, decide what *you* will do to change this.
2   Look at your last appraisal and compare your appraisal interview with the checklist. Did you and your appraiser get it right? If not, what do you need to do to get it right next time?
3   Look at your power-net. Who do you appraise? Look at some of the appraisals you have written for your subordinates? Are you getting it right? If not, decide what you need to do differently to get it right next time.

7 Consequence Assertion

Consequence Assertion is for very occasional use, and should be considered only when all other forms of assertion have been tried and have been unsuccessful and it is still essential that you do get your message across to the other person. It is the most potent form of assertion and therefore it is vital that it is carefully used.

You should ask yourself three questions when you are considering using it; make sure you can answer *yes* to all three:

1   Have I tried other forms of assertiveness which have not, so far, achieved their aim?
2   Do I have real sanctions which I am determined to apply unless there is a change in behaviour or actions?
3   Is there a *real* alternative outcome if the person concerned does listen and respond to my message?

Consequence Assertion means clearly pointing out the results of behaviour and actions and does not mean backing the other person into a corner and then attacking them.

It is important to use assertive body language and voice tones when using Consequence Assertion. Because your words are very powerful, an invasion of personal space, for example, finger-pointing, desk-bashing, and cold voice tones will convey aggression and destroy your chances of an assertive 'joint winners' solution. Your purpose should be to give a clear indication of the options and not to deliver a veiled threat!

Consequence Assertion is an effective way of dealing with a person with formal authority in relation to you, who has not responded to your previous use of, for example, Broken Record or Workable Compromise techniques.

Example

TRAINEE TO BOSS

'Although we have discussed the importance of my training programme and my concerns about my progress several times, I am still being regularly diverted from it to provide cover for daily staffing problems. Unless I am able to follow my schedule properly in the future, I will need to discuss it with the group training manager. I would much prefer to solve this at a local level.'

It can also be used to give an unequivocal signal to a fellow team member – for example somebody who is wearing a Hapless Harry mask.

> *'Your persistently poor timekeeping is causing problems for the rest of us; if you don't make a considerable, sustained improvement, I see no choice but to make a formal complaint, and I don't want to have to do that.'*

If you are an 'expert' in your power-net, you may have to use Consequence Assertion in order to illustrate clearly the results of inadvisable actions.

Example

> *'If you continue to ignore our health and safety policy in order to make cuts in the budget, I see no alternative but to start an internal review. I think we should reassess our business plan immediately to avoid this happening.'*

The most important message about Consequence Assertion is that you should not need to use it often if you are being effectively assertive; if you find you are using it often, it is a good indicator that you need to work harder at getting the alternative techniques right – ask yourself, am I being assertive or aggressive here? Use it only when it *is* vital that you get your message across and when the outcome is crucial. Remember that none of us can ever achieve *everything* we aim for – not every hand of cards has an ace – but we all need to feel good about the way we tried and confident enough to try again next time.

■ Practical exercises

■ *Exercise one*

1 Think about situations when the outcome was crucial or which ended unsatisfactorily for you. Use your power-net to recognise which people and what sorts of situations caused you the most difficulties.

2 Ask yourself what happened.

3 Ask yourself what might have happened if you had used Consequence Assertion – remember to ask yourself the three questions about the appropriateness of its use.

4 Identify where you might have been more successful using this approach – practise by talking through a script remembering your voice tone and body language.

■ *Exercise two*

Consequence Assertion is regularly misused, or used too often. Have you been too eager to jump to the last resort without working hard at the earlier stages? If yes, look at other ways you might have handled the situations – work out some assertive scripts which are less extreme than those you used.

Conclusion

At the beginning of this book we said that being assertive would bring many benefits both to organisations and to individuals. These can only come about if the many opportunities to use assertion are recognised and acted on.

Becoming comfortable and assured in using assertiveness takes time and effort. However, it is important to make a start. Every time you hold back and regret it or blow-up and feel guilty, is a potential assertive situation – you will only have a real chance to change negative outcomes if you change your behaviour. As important as positive outcomes is your own view of how you handled a situation. If you don't think well of yourself how can you expect the respect of others? So have a go, in small ways and in bigger ways.

The last words in this book must be assertive so:

We know that there is a lot to take in and it is not easy *however* we believe it to be enormously productive and rewarding so we suggest you plunge right in and practise *The business of Assertiveness.*

Summary of Exercises

Empathetic assertion: Practical exercises

■ *Exercise one: Active listening*

Active listening is a skill and can be developed. It involves total concentration in order to fully understand *what* is being said and *why* it is being said. It means:

- concentrating on the *issue* being discussed

- concentrating on the *thoughts around* the issue being discussed

- concentrating on the *feelings* that are being expressed

- concentrating on *omissions* – what is not being said – the 'hidden agenda', what thoughts and feelings are being suppressed or unrecognised

- concentrating on not instantly leaping to conclusions and *suspending judgement*

You can practise active listening on your own using a radio and cassette recorder, or a TV and video.

Choose a programme which involves people discussing personal issues, for example, an autobiographical interview and tape it. Time yourself for three minutes listening as carefully as you can to the programme. At the end of your time, transcribe in detail everything that you can remember. Active listening will have given you some insight into the issues, thoughts, feelings and emotions expressed, as well as a recognition of any omissions. Ask yourself, 'did I come to any conclusions during the three minutes?' If the answer is yes, ask yourself, 'was I listening accurately or was I judging?'

Then replay the tape and check your first listening – was it as active and accurate as it might have been? Do this as often as you can, and decide what helps you to listen well.

- Do you mentally picture images?

- Do you mentally summarise the main points?

- Do you remember key words? etc.

We often have a preference for ways of communicating; we have different ways of seeing the world. Recent studies in NLP (neuro linguistic programming) have suggested that some people like to express (and identify with) ideas through one of three different senses – touch, sight or hearing and that this can be indicated in their choice of language. Those with a preference for 'touch' or 'feeling', for example, use phrases like:

- 'Let's *take hold* of this problem and sort it out.'
- 'I think I *grasp* your meaning.'
- 'What I *feel* is going on here is . . .'
- 'Let's *toss* some ideas around.'
- 'You must *take* the bull by the horns.'
- 'In *concrete* terms it is a good deal.'
- 'Let's *put* our cards on the table.'

Others, however, are predominantly visual and would respond with (and tune in to) 'sight' words, for example:

- 'I *see* what you are saying.'
- 'There is a *clear* way through this problem.'
- '*Focus* on the important issue.'
- 'I can't believe my *eyes*.'
- 'We *see* eye to eye on this.'
- 'A great *image*.'
- 'This *looks* good.'

Some of us are auditory and would express themselves using 'hearing words', for example:

- 'We need to *tune* in to customer needs.'
- 'I'm *hearing* conflicting messages from you.'
- 'I can still *hear* him saying it.'
- 'There is a lot of *static* in the department about it.'
- '*Tell* it like it is.'
- '*Sounds* good.'
- 'It's *unheard* of.'
- 'Face the *music*.'
- 'In *harmony* with you.'

The key message from these studies seems to be that it can be helpful to recognise by active listening (as one method) which way of communicating a person uses and to match that way in any responses made.

■ *Exercise two: Practice*

Think about a situation or person you have handled recently in an unsatisfactory way, and which did not give you your desired outcome or happy ending. Analyse carefully what you did or did not do.

- Did I listen actively?
- Did I take time to let the other person know I understood what they were saying?
- Was I clear about my own thoughts and feelings?
- Did I express myself clearly?
- Did I have a clear picture of the outcome I wanted?

Now imagine yourself using the three steps to Empathetic Assertiveness. What would you say and do differently? Replay the scene mentally and try to envisage what reactions you may have had from the other person. It can sometimes help to write down your revised approach. Remember that using assertiveness can help you to buy time in a difficult situation, rather than feeling pressured to rush to an immediate and often hasty resolution.

Example

FINANCIAL CONTROLLER	I'm looking for an 11.5 per cent increase in sales on last year in the next period, and I'm relying on you to achieve that without increasing your staffing costs. I'm sure you'll be able to manage that.
SALES MANAGER	I understand that we have to meet tight targets in the next period; what I'd like to do, however, is to look in more detail at the effect of an 11.5 per cent sales increase on the staffing before I can give a realistic response. I'd like to talk to you again after I've done that. Could we meet at about 10.30 tomorrow morning?

- *Step One* – Actively listen to what is being said, and then show the other person that you both hear and understand what they are saying.

  'I understand that we have to meet tight targets in the next period.'

- *Step Two* – *Say what you think and feel.*

  'What I'd like to do, however, is to look in more detail at the effect of an 11.5 per cent sales increase on the staffing before I can give a realistic response.

- *Step Three* – *Say clearly what you want to happen.*

  'I'd like to talk to you again after I've done that, how about 10.30 tomorrow morning?'

If you have a friend or colleague you feel comfortable with, brief them on the situation you've thought through, and ask them to role-play the opposite person. Measure their reactions to your assertiveness and keep working until you feel happy with the solution you've worked out.

■ *Exercise three: Observation*

Observe and listen to a discussion/disagreement between two people (real or portrayed by actors on TV or radio) who are not being assertive – they may be being aggressive or passive, or a combination of both. Recognise where the key opportunities for assertive behaviour and solutions are being missed. Imagine or write out an alternative assertive script i.e. what might have happened had one or both parties followed the three steps. Observe and analyse your own actions, and those of others, as often as you can; decide how effective you are being, take note of what you find difficult to do and note the areas you want to improve further. When you become confident you may well find your assertive skills will transform your life and your potential.

Body language: Practical exercises

■ *Exercise one: People-watching*

Practise 'people-watching' and interpret the signals they give – how are assertive people using their bodies? Look at people who are being aggressive – what is mirrored in their body language? Look at passive people – how do their bodies reinforce their verbal behaviour?

Particularly revealing situations can be where people are in a public place and don't know each other. Watch the person on the train who spreads over two seats deliberately to gain more room, and then watch how other people looking for a seat approach to ask if this one is free. Watch the different body language signals given to a queue jumper!

■ *Exercise two: Interpretating body language*

Videotape an interview on television but watch the scene with the volume *off*; try to interpret what is being said and how the people are feeling by reading their body language. Check how accurate you have been by replaying the tape with the volume on.

■ *Exercise three: The body language of the office*

Look at your workplace with a fresh objective eye. How do people use their offices and furniture to give signals? Are desks used as barriers or defences; is there an option to sit informally in relaxing chairs? Does everyone operate behind constantly closed doors? How do you use your office? Are you giving the signals that you want to? Your workplace is an extension of yourself – is it how you want it to be?

■ *Exercise four: You and your body language*

Using a mirror, check your usual body posture. Stand in a way in which you feel comfortable – this is probably how you usually stand. Is it an assertive posture? Sitting in an upright position, bend your head slightly to one side, and then to the other. Which side feels more comfortable to you? Be aware that the 'comfortable' position is probably the one you use when you are being passive, and trying to plead for something, or make excuses for something. Remember that a firm upright head position will help you to be assertive. Decide if you need to practise adapting your posture. Still using a mirror, practise asking a question or saying something which you would normally find difficult to do assertively. Keep practising until you find the most effective body language to reinforce your verbal skills.

■ *Exercise five: Voice control*

Practise controlling your voice tone by reading sections of your daily newspaper aloud. Try reading the Birth and Death columns to provide you with two extremes; find a humorous article and a

Body language is more than just your body.

serious article and try them. Find some poetry that moves you, and practise reading it out loud. Write out things that you find difficult to express and practise until you find the right tones.

Broken record: Practical exercises

■ *Exercise one*

Analyse your power-nets – is there anyone who regularly does not listen to you? Anyone who never takes your ideas/suggestions on board? Practise the Broken Record technique before and during your next encounter with them.

■ *Exercise two*

Ask a friend to play the part of a very persistent salesperson, using every possible ploy to sell into your company and to get you interested in the product. You should use the Broken Record technique to get across the message that you are not interested.

■ *Exercise three*

Listen to TV and radio interviews, particularly those involving politicians, identifying when either the interviewer or politician uses the Broken Record technique to get their view across. Notice when it is used effectively, and contrast this with occasions when whining or stonewalling takes over.

Saying no: Practical exercise

Use your power-nets to think about what kinds of things you find it hard to say no to and what kinds of requests and people are hard to refuse? For example, is it hard for you to refuse personal favours, social invitations, impossible demands at work?

Is it hard for you to say no to your boss, your peers, your team, your partner, your neighbour, or your children?

Makes lists under these two headings 'It is hard to refuse . . .' and 'It is hard to say no to . . .'. Ask a friend to ask some tough favours of you, role-playing your difficult people and invitations. Practise saying no.

Workable compromise: Practical exercise

How to develop your workable compromise approach

Identify – at work, in your personal life, and as an observer of local/national/world politics – situations that seem unworkable and where there is no movement between two solutions. Brainstorm until you arrive at real alternatives.

Positive inner dialogue: Practical exercises

■ *Exercise one*

Get what is in, out. It is amazing how effective it can be to voice your own fears. Have a dialogue with yourself or with a trusted friend or colleague when you recognise that your inner thoughts are leading you into an anxiety trap.

OUTER   What is it that's making you feel so anxious?
INNER   I'm concerned about the presentation I'm going to give to the executive meeting tomorrow, I'm sure it's going to be a disaster.

OUTER	Why is it going to be a disaster, haven't you done any work for it?
INNER	Yes, I've worked for hours on it, I'm just so nervous I know I'm going to blow it.
OUTER	Well, if you've worked for hours on it you must be satisfied with the material that you've prepared.
INNER	Oh, yes, it isn't the material, it's the thought of having to stand up and talk to these people, it's just terrifying.
OUTER	Right, the material is good so it's just getting over the nerves. I thought you knew these people.
INNER	Yes, I've met them individually and that was fine, but in a group – that's a different matter.
OUTER	So, you know that these people are reasonable and that they will want to hear what you've got to say.
INNER	Yes, that is true, but I've got all the technical details to handle as well and I'm useless on technical details . . . I've got to do the video and the overhead projector . . . I've got to get all the timings right . . .
OUTER	Okay, so today you can run through all the technical details to iron out any wrinkles before tomorrow. You'll then be well prepared and ready for anything. You know you're good at handling problems or questions off the cuff, so look at it as an opportunity to really perform well and get your message across effectively.

■ *Exercise two*

It can sometimes help to put yourself through the worst case test. This helps to put your anticipated problem into perspective.

INNER	I know this presentation is going to be a disaster, I'd do anything not to be here.
OUTER	Okay, so even if it is a disaster, what is the worst thing that could happen to you as a result?
INNER	Well, it could be the ruin of me.
OUTER	How would it be the ruin of you?
INNER	I could be fired.
OUTER	How likely is it that you're going to be fired? When was the last time that someone was fired for a bad presentation?
INNER	Well, I don't know . . .

OUTER	Even if you are fired is that the end of your world? Is this the only job you could ever do?
INNER	No, but my whole career would be finished.
OUTER	Why would it be finished? You've always said you'd like to do something completely different.
INNER	Yes, but I want to be a success in this job, not a failure.
OUTER	Fine, so concentrate on your successes and stop worrying about possible failures – go for it! The worst is not nearly as bad as you imagine it is.

Fogging: Practical exercises

■ *Exercise one*

- Look at your power-net.

- Is there someone who regularly deals with problems by attacking you?

- What invalid criticisms do they make of you?

- Practise retrospective Fogging – how else could you have replied?

■ *Exercise two*

Make two lists for yourself – one of criticisms which are valid, one of criticisms which are not. Ask a friend to give you feedback from both lists in an aggressive way – this will help you practise making choices about Fogging – whether you use it to simply calm down the situation and remain uninvolved, or whether you need to use it to pave the way towards Workable Compromise. Either way you need to deal with it.

INSULT	FOG
'I can't believe you chose that outfit! The colour is all wrong.'	'Yes, taste is such a personal thing, isn't it?'
'How come your office always looks like a disaster area?'	'Yes, isn't it interesting how people work differently?'

Consequence assertion: Practical exercises

■ *Exercise one*

1 Think about situations when the outcome was crucial, which ended unsatisfactorily for you. Use your power-net to recognise which people and what sorts of situations cause you the most difficulties.

2 Ask yourself what happened.

3 Ask yourself what might have happened if you had used Consequence Assertion – remember to ask yourself the three questions about the appropriateness of its use.

4 Identify where you might have been more successful using this approach – practise by talking through a script remembering your voice tone and body language.

■ *Exercise two*

Consequence Assertion is regularly misused, or used too often. Have you been too eager to jump to the last resort without working hard at the earlier stages? If yes, look at other ways you might have handled the situations – work out some assertive scripts which are less extreme than those you used.

Bibliography

Assertiveness at Work *Ken and Kate Back* McGraw-Hill, 1982

Games People Play *Eric Berne* Penguin, 1982

A Woman in Your Own Right *Ann Dickson* Quartet, 1982

I'm O.K., You're O.K. *Thomas Harris* Pan, 1973

Staying O.K. *Amy and Thomas Harris* Pan, 1986

The Right to be You *Nancy Paul* Chartwell Bratt/Studen litteratur, 1985

When I say No I feel Guilty *Manuel J. Smith* Bantam, 1975

Working Choices *Rennie Fritchie and Jane Skinner* J.M. Dent

Ask for the Moon and Get It *Percy Ross with Dick Samson* Thorsons, 1989

Tutor's guides

Career Life Planning – Tutor's Guide by *Fritchie/Ryan*

Interpersonal Skills for Women Managers – Tutor's Guide *Thorne/Fritchie*

Women, Work and Training – A Resource Manual for Trainers *Smith/Fritchie/Smith*

Working with Assertiveness, *Rennie Fritchie*, BBC, 1988 (Pack contains 2 video cassettes and a student's guide)

BUSINESS MATTERS MANAGEMENT GUIDES

A series of practical self-help book and tape packs bringing tried and tested management techniques to a wide range of people. Each book is accessible and jargon-free and is accompanied by a C50 tape.

GIVE AND TAKE

A Practical Guide to Making the Most of Meetings

Jack Gratus

MANAGING PRESSURE AT WORK

Helen Froggatt and Paul Stamp

SPEAK FOR YOURSELF

A Practical Guide to Speaking with Confidence

John Campbell

DOING BUSINESS IN ...

A First-Class Series for Business People who are Going Places!

For today's mobile businessman or woman. All the back-up that you need to operate successfully abroad: from marketing to the law and national character to business etiquette. If you are an executive dealing with the continent of Europe, make *Doing Business In . . .* your passport to success!

The first titles in the series are:

DOING BUSINESS IN EASTERN EUROPE
Karen Liebreich

DOING BUSINESS IN ITALY
Dalbert Hallenstein

For further details of the titles
listed overleaf and other BBC
Books write to:

BBC Books
Enquiry Service (BM)
Room A3116
Woodlands
80 Wood Lane
London, W12 0TT

All BBC Books are available
through good bookshops.